C

New Wave English Skills Practice

Revised edition

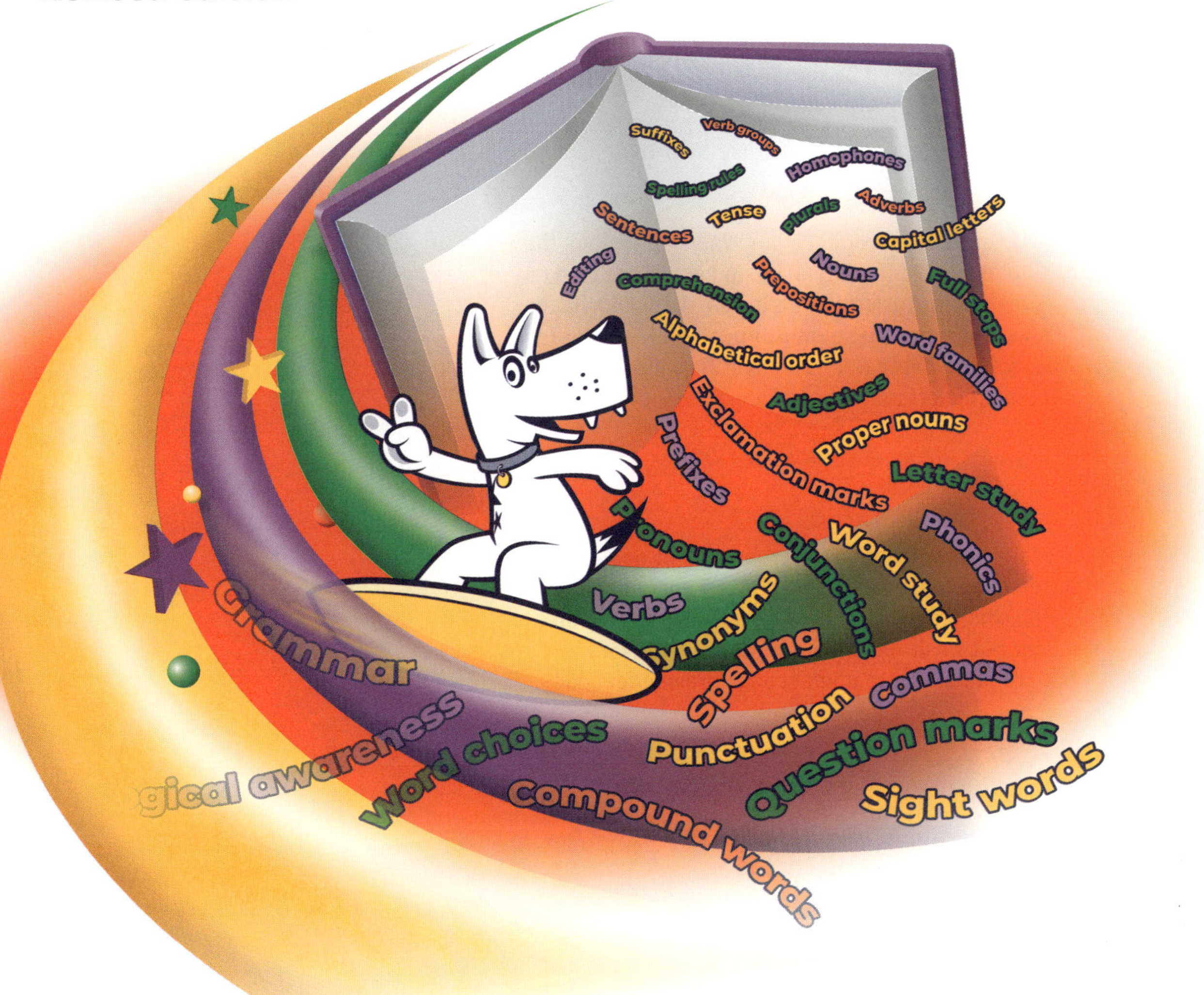

This book belongs to:

New wave English skills practice *(Book C)*

Published by R.I.C. Publications® 2014

Revised and reprinted 2022
Reprinted 2023, 2024, 2025
ISBN 978-1-922843-56-2
RIC–6222

Titles available in this series:
New wave English skills practice *(Book A)*
New wave English skills practice *(Book B)*
New wave English skills practice *(Book C)*
New wave English skills practice *(Book D)*
New wave English skills practice *(Book E)*
New wave English skills practice *(Book F)*

R.I.C. Publications® follows the guidelines for punctuation and grammar as recommended by the *Style manual for authors, editors and printers*, 2002, 6th edn.

Note, however, that teachers should use their own guide if there is a conflict.

R.I.C. Publications® acknowledges the Wadjak people of the Nyoongar Nation as the Traditional Custodians of the land on which our Western Australian office is based. We acknowledge the Traditional Custodians of Country throughout Australia and pay our respects to Elders past and present. R.I.C. Publications® recognises the role of First Nations Elders as Australia's first educators.

R.I.C. Publications®
PO Box 332
Greenwood
Western Australia 6924
+61 8 9240 9888
ricpublications.com.au
mail@ricpublications.com.au

FOREWORD

In this daily practice workbook you will be able to develop your ability to use English. Each day, you will have questions to answer in the areas of spelling, word study, punctuation and grammar. There are 160 days of questions in this workbook.

Seven weeks of each unit begin with a new skill focus. This will help remind you of some of the skills and terminology that will be used throughout the workbook. Every day, two questions will focus on the skill that is introduced at the start of the week. The remaining questions will be mixed practice which will help to improve your English skills as well as your knowledge about how language works.

At the completion of each unit, you will have the opportunity to review what you have learnt by doing one day of skill focus revision questions. Your daily scores are recorded in the bubble at the bottom of each day. These daily scores can be transferred onto the record sheets at the front of your book.

This will give an overview of your performance for the whole school year. Be sure to read each question carefully before you answer it. If you find a question too difficult, move on to the next one. If you have time at the end, you can go back to the one you haven't done.

CONTENTS

Record sheet

Week 1		Week 2		Week 3		Week 4	
Date		*Date*		*Date*		*Date*	
Skill focus		Skill focus		Skill focus		Skill focus	
Day 1		Day 1		Day 1		Day 1	
Day 2		Day 2		Day 2		Day 2	
Day 3		Day 3		Day 3		Day 3	
Day 4		Day 4		Day 4		Day 4	
Day 5		Day 5		Day 5		Day 5	

Week 5		Week 6		Week 7		Week 8	
Date		*Date*		*Date*		*Date*	
Skill focus		Skill focus		Skill focus		Day 1	
Day 1		Day 1		Day 1		Day 2	
Day 2		Day 2		Day 2		Day 3	
Day 3		Day 3		Day 3		Day 4	
Day 4		Day 4		Day 4		Day 5	
Day 5		Day 5		Day 5		Revision	

Week 9		Week 10		Week 11		Week 12	
Date		*Date*		*Date*		*Date*	
Skill focus		Skill focus		Skill focus		Skill focus	
Day 1		Day 1		Day 1		Day 1	
Day 2		Day 2		Day 2		Day 2	
Day 3		Day 3		Day 3		Day 3	
Day 4		Day 4		Day 4		Day 4	
Day 5		Day 5		Day 5		Day 5	

Week 13		Week 14		Week 15		Week 16	
Date		*Date*		*Date*		*Date*	
Skill focus		Skill focus		Skill focus		Day 1	
Day 1		Day 1		Day 1		Day 2	
Day 2		Day 2		Day 2		Day 3	
Day 3		Day 3		Day 3		Day 4	
Day 4		Day 4		Day 4		Day 5	
Day 5		Day 5		Day 5		Revision	

Record sheet

Week 17		Week 18		Week 19		Week 20	
Date		*Date*		*Date*		*Date*	
Skill focus		Skill focus		Skill focus		Skill focus	
Day 1		Day 1		Day 1		Day 1	
Day 2		Day 2		Day 2		Day 2	
Day 3		Day 3		Day 3		Day 3	
Day 4		Day 4		Day 4		Day 4	
Day 5		Day 5		Day 5		Day 5	

Week 21		Week 22		Week 23		Week 24	
Date		*Date*		*Date*		*Date*	
Skill focus		Skill focus		Skill focus		Day 1	
Day 1		Day 1		Day 1		Day 2	
Day 2		Day 2		Day 2		Day 3	
Day 3		Day 3		Day 3		Day 4	
Day 4		Day 4		Day 4		Day 5	
Day 5		Day 5		Day 5		Revision	

Week 25		Week 26		Week 27		Week 28	
Date		*Date*		*Date*		*Date*	
Skill focus		Skill focus		Skill focus		Skill focus	
Day 1		Day 1		Day 1		Day 1	
Day 2		Day 2		Day 2		Day 2	
Day 3		Day 3		Day 3		Day 3	
Day 4		Day 4		Day 4		Day 4	
Day 5		Day 5		Day 5		Day 5	

Week 29		Week 30		Week 31		Week 32	
Date		*Date*		*Date*		*Date*	
Skill focus		Skill focus		Skill focus		Day 1	
Day 1		Day 1		Day 1		Day 2	
Day 2		Day 2		Day 2		Day 3	
Day 3		Day 3		Day 3		Day 4	
Day 4		Day 4		Day 4		Day 5	
Day 5		Day 5		Day 5		Revision	

WEEK 1

Skill focus

Types of sentences

Did you know that there are different types of sentences?

Each sentence has a different purpose.

All sentences start with a capital letter, but they might end with a full stop, question mark or exclamation mark.

The type of punctuation mark used depends on the type of sentence:

Statements

Statements are sentences that tell you about something.

My aunt visited me today and brought me a new book.

Commands

Commands are sentences that tell you to do something.

Ask your brother what he wants for lunch.

Statements and **commands** that show a strong feeling end with an exclamation mark.

Questions

Questions are sentences that ask you something.

Would you like to go shopping with me after school?

No matter the purpose, all sentences must start with a capital letter and end with a punctuation mark.

Practice questions

1. Add punctuation to the end of the sentence.

   Where did you leave your bicycle helmet ☐

2. Punctuate. ***?*** or ***!***

   Watch out for the car ☐

Day 1

1. Add punctuation to the end of the sentence.

   My baby sister drinks milk from a bottle ☐

2. Punctuate. ***?*** or ***!***

   Where is my glue ☐

3. Rewrite the misspelt word.

   You shud come over to play today. ☐

4. Write the plural form of ***car***. *Hint: plural means more than one.*

   ☐

5. Count the vowels (a, e, i, o, u) and consonants. ***Wednesday***

   vowels ☐ consonants ☐

6. Add ***un*** to make the opposite.

   ☐friendly

7. Add ***ing*** and ***ed*** to make two new words.

   play ☐ ☐

8. Which word means an ***ocean***?

   see sea

9. Circle the word closest in meaning to ***little***.

   big small huge

10. Circle the opposite of ***back***.

    front find behind

11. Circle the two rhyming words.

    trick shock brick

12. ***is*** or ***are***?

    My friends ☐ *visiting tomorrow.*

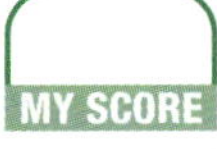

Day 2

1. This sentence is a command ☐ or a question ☐?

   What time is it?

2. Punctuate. **?** or **.**

   I have two brothers ☐

3. Rewrite the misspelt word.

   Next yeer my family will go to China for a holiday.

   ☐

4. Write the singular form of ***streets***. *Hint: singular means only one.*

   ☐

5. Count the vowels (a, e, i, o, u) and consonants. ***January***

   vowels ☐ consonants ☐

6. Add ***un*** to make the opposite.

   ☐tie

7. Add ***y*** to make a new word.

   grass ask ☐

8. Circle the correct word.

   I have to/too/two hands.

9. Circle the word closest in meaning to ***kind***.

   nice mean strong

10. Circle the opposite of ***high***.

    tall low below

11. Circle the two rhyming words.

    catch witch match

12. ***has*** or ***have***?

    I ☐ *two cats and a dog.*

MY SCORE

Day 3

WEEK 1

1. Add punctuation to the end of the sentence.

   What is the fastest way to your house ☐

2. Punctuate. **?** or **!**

   Go away ☐

3. Write the jumbled word correctly.

   I ouwld like to visit Rome.

   ☐

4. Write the plural form of ***dress***.

   ☐

5. Count the vowels (a, e, i, o, u) and consonants. ***buying***

   vowels ☐ consonants ☐

6. Add two letters to make the opposite of this word.

   ☐ripe

7. Add ***ing*** and ***ed*** to make two new words.

   pant ☐ ☐

8. Which word means a buzzy insect?

   be bee

9. Circle the word closest in meaning to ***many***.

   none lots few

10. Circle the opposite of ***front***.

    top back bottom

11. Circle the rhyming words.

    walk warm talk

12. ***is*** or ***are***?

    She ☐ *very tall.*

MY SCORE

WEEK 1

Day 4

1. This sentence is a command ☐ or a question ☐?

   Close the door!

2. Punctuate. **?** or **.**

   Pass the salt, please ☐

3. Add the word with the correct spelling. ***coold could***

   Erin said I ☐ *borrow her pencil.*

4. Write the singular form of ***benches***.

5. Count the vowels (a, e, i, o, u) and consonants. ***science***

   vowels ☐ consonants ☐

6. Add two letters to make the opposite of this word.

   ☐fair

7. Add ***y*** to make a new word.

   wind told ☐

8. Which word? ***bye buy by***

   I passed ☐ *your house today.*

9. Circle the word closest in meaning to ***father***.

   mother dad uncle

10. Circle the opposite of ***quick***.

    fast slow walk

11. Circle the rhyming words.

    paddle middle riddle

12. ***has*** or ***have***?

    He ☐ *a big house.*

MY SCORE

Day 5

1. Add a punctuation mark.

   Did you see the hot air balloon ☐

2. Punctuate. **?** or **!**

   How are you ☐

3. Rewrite the misspelt word.

   Every nite we eat dinner at the table. ☐

4. Write the plural of ***sport***.

5. Count the vowels (a, e, i, o, u) and consonants. ***heart***

   vowels ☐ consonants ☐

6. Add two letters to make the opposite of this word.

   ☐done

7. Add ***ing*** and ***ed*** to make two new words.

   wind ☐ ☐

8. ***fore*** or ***for***?

   What shall we have ☐ *lunch?*

9. Circle two words that are close in meaning.

   hurry wait rush

10. Which word is NOT close in meaning to ***soar***?

    fly glide crash

11. Circle the word you can add to ***some***.

    thing self

12. ***did*** or ***done***?

    He has ☐ *a really good job.*

MY SCORE

Nouns and proper nouns

Nouns are the names given to people, places and things.

They tell us who, what and where in a sentence.

We can separate nouns in to two groups.

Some nouns are **common nouns**. They are the general names for people, places and things:

Proper nouns name specific people, places and things. They start with a capital letter.

You can remember which nouns and other words need a capital letter using the '**MINTS**' acronym:

M: Months, days and holidays

I: The word 'I'

N: Names of people and places

T: Titles of people, films, books and other things

S: Start of sentences

Practice questions

1. Circle the noun.

   We walked quickly to the park.

2. Add capital letters for the proper nouns.

   We bought our dog bruno from a man in perth.

1. Circle the noun.

   My dog is cute.

2. Add capital letters for the proper nouns.

   When my family goes to spain, we will stay in madrid.

3. Rewrite the misspelt word correctly.

   Brush your teeth befour bed. ☐

4. Write the singular form of ***cousins***.

   ☐

5. Add two letters to make this word mean the opposite.

   ☐likely

6. ***four*** or ***for?***

   The trip took about ☐ *hours.*

7. Circle two words that are close in meaning.

   rained snowed sprinkled

8. Circle the opposites.

   some less more

9. Circle the rhyming words.

   try kite high

10. Which punctuation mark? **. ! ?**

    Run☐

11. Add punctuation.

    many lemons and oranges had fallen from the trees

12. ***has***, ***have*** or ***having***?

    My sister ☐ *to do a lot of homework.*

WEEK 2

Day 2

1. Circle the proper noun.

   I live in Iceland.

2. Add capital letters for the proper nouns.

   I saw kate's dog, samson, on wednesday.

3. Write the jumbled word correctly.

   We were the last ones to ordab the bus.

4. Circle the plural form of ***watch***.

   watches watchs watch

5. What is the correct spelling for ***crawl*** + ***ing***?

6. Circle the word that sounds the same as ***nose***.

   knows nows

7. Circle the word that means 60 seconds.

   hour minute

8. Circle the opposites.

   war peace love

9. Circle the rhyming words.

   another father mother

10. Punctuate. **?** or **!**

    Where is your sister

11. Circle the missing punctuation mark. **. ! ?**

    I went to see the doctor this morning

12. ***did*** or ***done***?

    Sam has all of her work.

MY SCORE

Day 3

1. Circle the noun.

   That bin smells!

2. Add capital letters for the proper nouns.

   Yesterday was tuesday, the first of september.

3. Write the jumbled word correctly.

   The Inkabet on my bed keeps me very warm.

4. Write the plural of ***vegetable***.

5. Add two letters to make this word mean the opposite.

   able

6. Put ***rode*** and ***road*** in the correct places.

   Jo her new bike on the .

7. Circle the word that means ***commenced***.

   began ended

8. The opposite of ***hot*** is .

9. Circle the word that rhymes with ***flood***.

   filled blood killed

10. Which punctuation mark? **. ! ?**

    Bring that to me, please

11. Punctuate.

    spring is my favourite season

12. ***was*** or ***were***?

    Yesterday very rainy and cold.

MY SCORE

Day 4

1. Circle the proper noun.

   My uncle lives in Cairns.

2. Add capital letters for the proper nouns.

   Australia has school holidays in december and january.

3. Add the word with the correct spelling. ***becos*** ***because***

   I was happy ______ *it was my birthday.*

4. Write the singular form of ***uncles***. ______

5. What is the correct spelling for ***hear*** + ***ing***?

   ______

6. Put ***night*** and ***knight*** in the correct places.

   The brave ______ *rode off into the* ______ *on his horse.*

7. Circle the word closest in meaning to ***blank***.

   full   empty   writing

8. The opposite of ***day*** is ______.

9. Circle the word that rhymes with ***done***.

   harm   none   does

10. Punctuate. ***?*** or ***!***   *What's this* ☐

11. Circle the missing punctuation mark. **.** ***!*** ***?***

    Look out

12. ***is*** or ***are***?

    You ______ *taller than Bob.*

MY SCORE

Day 5

WEEK 2

1. Circle the noun.

   Oranges are very juicy.

2. Add capital letters for the proper nouns.

   Mum and emma caught the train from melbourne to geelong.

3. Rewrite the underlined word correctly.

   Don't say that. It's not <u>trew</u>! ______

4. Write the plural form of ***box***. ______

5. Add two letters to make this word mean the opposite.

   ☐do

6. Put ***here*** and ***hear*** in the correct places.

   I can't ______ *you from over* ______.

7. Circle the word closest in meaning to ***chair***.

   sit   seat   stand

8. The opposite of ***before*** is ______.

9. Circle two rhyming words.

   ghost   nose   goes

10. Which punctuation mark? **.** ***!*** ***?***

    Are you hungry ☐

11. Add punctuation.

    english is spoken in many countries around the world

12. ***was*** or ***were***?

    They ______ *a great team!*

MY SCORE

Skill focus

Verbs and tense

Verbs are words that show an action:

think *bring* *go*

Every sentence needs a verb.

Verbs can tell us about:

- what is happening now (in the **present**);
- what has happened in the **past**; and
- what will happen in the **future**.

This is called **tense**.

Endings like ***ing*** or ***ed*** are usually added to verbs to show their tense:

*I **played** at the park yesterday. I can hear children **playing** there now.*

However, some verbs become a different word when we change their tense:

*I want to **eat** a cookie. My sister already **ate** one.*

Practice questions

1. Circle the verb.

   The dog caught the ball.

2. Circle the past tense form of ***count***.

   counted counting counts

Day 1

1. Circle the verb.

   I ran in a race.

2. Circle the past tense form of ***jump***.

   jumping jumped jumper

3. Circle and rewrite the misspelt word.

   I kno my ten times table.

4. Write the singular form of ***foxes***.

5. Add ***y*** to make a new word.

   sand kick

6. Write the correct word.

   sauce source

   I don't like tomato ______.

7. Circle the word closest in meaning to ***enormous***.

   small captured huge

8. The opposite of ***first*** is ______.

9. Punctuate. ***?*** or ***!***

   Get down

10. Circle the word that needs a capital letter.

    russia father mother

11. Circle the noun.

    They were eating apples.

12. Circle the proper noun.

    I go to basketball training every Thursday.

Day 2

1. Circle the verb.

   I play football.

2. Circle the tense this sentence is written in. ***past*** ***present*** ***future***

   Yesterday, I went to my friend's house.

3. Circle and rewrite the jumbled word.

   Stand in reodr from shortest to tallest. [ ]

4. Circle the plural of ***dollar***.

   dollars dollares

5. Add two letters to make this word mean the opposite.

   [ ]afraid

6. ***to***, ***too*** or ***two***?

   Let's go [ ] *the beach.*

7. Circle the word closest in meaning to ***furious***.

   happy excellent angry

8. Write the opposite of ***inside***.

   [ ]

9. Punctuate. ***?*** or ***!*** *Watch out*[ ]

10. Add punctuation to the end of the sentence.

    Tomorrow, I will go shopping with my sister[ ]

11. Circle the missing noun. ***beans*** ***carrot***

    Rory picked ______ *from the garden.*

12. Circle two nouns.

    We rode our bikes to school yesterday.

MY SCORE

Day 3

WEEK 3

1. Circle the verb.

   I fell on the rocks.

2. Circle a present tense form of ***walked***.

   walkest walks walker

3. Add the word with the correct spelling. ***during*** ***juring***

   The rude lady talked [ ] *the film.*

4. Circle the plural of ***kiss***.

   kisses kisss

5. Add ***y*** to make a new word.

   swim wind [ ]

6. Put ***eye*** and ***I*** in the correct places.

   '[ ] *spy, with my little* [ ]' *is a game.*

7. Circle the close meanings.

   woman man lady

8. Circle the opposite of ***sweet***.

   bitter noisy short

9. Punctuate. ***?*** or ***!***

   Where's Dad going[ ]

10. Add four capital letters.

    the swan river is in perth.

11. Circle the noun.

    Our team plays very well.

12. Circle the proper noun.

    I live in Sydney.

Day 4

1. Circle the verb.

   We bought a new car last week.

2. Circle the tense this sentence is written in. ***past*** ***present*** ***future***

   The ship sank on the dangerous reef.

3. Add the word with the correct spelling. ***climb*** ***clime***

   Can you [ ] *to the top of the ladder?*

4. Circle the plural form of ***latch***.

   latches latchs

5. Add two letters to make this word mean the opposite.

   [ ]changed

6. ***by*** or ***buy***?

   I need to [ ] *some new socks.*

7. Circle the close meanings.

   child baby adult

8. Circle the opposite of ***asleep***.

   sleepy awake dream

9. Punctuate. ***?*** or ***!***

   Can I help you[ ]

10. Add punctuation to the end of the sentence.

    Let the dog out when you get home[ ]

11. Circle the missing noun.
    noodle ***vegetable*** ***rice***

    Ross boiled the _____ *in the pot.*

12. Circle the noun.

    She stepped on broken glass.

Day 5

1. Circle the verb.

   Throw me the ball, please.

2. Circle the past tense form of ***sleep***.

   sleeped sleepy slept

3. Rewrite the underlined word correctly.

   Do you know where <u>evryone</u> is?

   [ ]

4. Write the plural of ***match***.

   [ ]

5. Add ***y*** to make a new word.

   fall bump [ ]

6. Write the correct word. ***won*** ***one***

   I [ ] *a trophy for running.*

7. Circle the word that means a place to watch a dramatic play.

   cinema theatre

8. Circle the opposite of ***take***.

   give present steal

9. Punctuate. ***?*** or ***!***

   Who's next, please[ ]

10. Circle the word that needs a capital letter.

    monkey christmas television

11. Circle the noun.

    He was a great acrobat.

12. Circle the proper noun.

    My uncle is from France.

Adjectives

Some words help us describe the people, places or things in sentences.

These words are called **adjectives**.

Adjectives can come before or after the noun they are describing:

The ***hairy spider*** *crawled across the girl's arm.*

Mum was angry because my ***clothes*** *were* ***filthy****.*

The endings ***er*** or ***est*** are often added to the end of an adjective.

This helps compare two or more things.

A kitten is small.

A mouse is smaller.

An ant is the smallest.

Practice questions

1. Circle the adjective.

   The children played in the beautiful garden.

2. Write the adjective in the correct form. ***dark***

   We closed the curtains to make the room ______ .

1. Circle the adjective.

   Dad has a beautiful garden.

2. Write the adjective in the correct form. ***light***

   A feather is ______ *than a brick.*

3. Add the word with the correct spelling. ***sqware*** ***square***

   A ______ *has four sides.*

4. Change this verb into the past tense.

   talk ______

5. Which word can you add to ***some***?

   thing self

6. Circle the rhyming word. ***crowd***

   crown loud mouth

7. Which word does NOT have a similar meaning to ***gigantic***?

   giant huge tiny

8. ***go***, ***goes*** or ***gone***?

   She's already ______ .

9. Add four capital letters.

   yesterday, i visited john in manly.

10. Write the missing noun. ***tunnel*** ***bridge***

    We drove across the old ______ *to get home.*

11. Write the missing verb. ***draw*** ***drew***

    When we get back, I'll ______ *a picture.*

12. Change the verb and rewrite it in the past tense.

    We walk to school.

    ______

WEEK 4

Day 2

1. Circle the adjective.

   Samson is a massive dog.

2. Change the ending to make this word mean the most small.

   smaller [ ]

3. Add the word with the correct spelling. ***circle cercle***

   To play duck-duck-goose you must sit in a [ ].

4. Add the correct form of ***blame*** to the sentence.

   My brother is always [ ] *me for everything!*

5. Add ***er*** to make a new word.

   last fast [ ]

6. Which word means ***correct***?

   write right

7. Circle the opposite of ***throw***.

   shoot catch hit

8. ***is*** or ***are***?

   We [ ] *going on holiday next month.*

9. Add three capital letters.

   my brother, jason, was born in july.

10. Add the missing noun. ***hoops sticks***

    My dog likes to jump through [ ].

11. Circle the tense this sentence is written in. ***past present future***

    I walk to school every day.

12. ***he's*** or ***his***?

    I think [ ] *rude.*

MY SCORE

Day 3

1. Circle the adjective.

   The squid we caught was slimy.

2. Write the adjective in the correct form. ***tall***

   You are not much [ ] *than I am.*

3. Circle and rewrite the misspelt word.

   I saw a goanna on the golf corse. [ ]

4. Change this verb into the past tense.

   cover [ ]

5. Which word can you add to ***every***?

   times thing

6. Circle the rhyming words.

   reason person season

7. Which word is NOT an opposite of ***mean***?

   nice nasty kind

8. ***go***, ***goes*** or ***gone***?

   Where should we [ ]*?*

9. Add three capital letters.

   I saw amy and kate on wednesday.

10. Write the missing noun. ***game netball toys***

    On Thursdays, I play [ ].

11. Write the missing verb. ***watch watches***

    I [ ] *TV most afternoons.*

12. Change the verb and rewrite it in the past tense.

    We buy chocolate.

    [ ]

MY SCORE

WEEK 4

Day 4

1. Circle the two adjectives.

   The girl's hair was long and shiny.

2. Change the ending to make this word mean the most quiet.

   quieter [ ]

3. Circle and rewrite the misspelt word.

   'What is duble two?' my granny asked. [ ]

4. Add the correct form of ***die*** to the sentence.

   I was really upset when my cat [ ].

5. Add ***er*** to make a new word.

   strong weight [ ]

6. Which word means ***letters***?

   male mail

7. Circle the opposite of ***go***.

   play move stop

8. ***is*** or ***are***?

   She [ ] *a very friendly person.*

9. Add four capital letters.

   i live near the river nile in cairo.

10. Circle the missing noun.
    chocolate sauce

    I ate too much ______ *after dinner last night.*

11. Circle the tense this sentence is written in. ***past present future***

    I came second in the race.

12. ***his*** or ***he's***?

    I saw [ ] *parents drive past.*

Day 5

1. Circle the two adjectives.

   There was a dangerous snake in the long grass.

2. Write the adjective in the correct form. ***kind***

   I have the [ ] *mum.*

3. Circle and rewrite the misspelt word.

   I have two eyes and a mowth. [ ]

4. Change the verb to the present tense.

   ran [ ]

5. Circle the word you can add to ***bed***.

   blanket room

6. Circle the rhyming word. ***cheap***

   cheat sleep meet

7. Which word does NOT have a similar meaning to ***stare***?

   look watch listen

8. ***go***, ***goes*** or ***gone***?

   Our car [ ] *fast.*

9. Add two capital letters.

   let's go to mandurah tomorrow.

10. Write the missing noun.
    roast sausages

    We had a [ ] *for dinner.*

11. Write the missing verb. ***fly flew***

    We [ ] *to Spain to visit family last year.*

12. Change the verb and rewrite it in the past tense.

    They eat too much.

    [ ]

Skill focus

Rules for adding endings

Sometimes, endings are added to words to make new words.

This changes the meaning of the **base word**.

A base word is a word that doesn't have any word parts added to it.

Often, the base word does not change when we add the ending:

play: playing played player

For other words, there are rules we must remember when we add an ending.

Base word ending in consonant then *y*

Change ***y*** to ***i*** then add the ending: copy + ed = copied

We don't do this when we add ***ing***.

Base word ending with silent *e*

Drop the ***e*** then add the ending: stripe + y = stripy

One syllable base word ending with a short vowel (a, e, i, o, u) sound then consonant

Double the consonant before adding the ending: hop(+p)ing = hopping

Practice questions

1. What is the base word of ***coloured*** and ***colouring***?

2. ***copy*** + ***ing*** =

Day 1

1. What is the base word of ***added*** and ***adding***?

2. ***shine*** + ***y*** =

3. Add the word with the correct spelling. ***seeson*** ***season***

   Spring is my favourite ______.

4. Circle the past tense form of ***go***.

   gode went goed

5. Which one is not a word?

   sleeping wenting running

6. Circle the rhyming words.

   power crowd flower

7. ***four*** or ***for***?

   Is it ______ *o'clock already?*

8. Use ***come*** or ***coming*** in the sentence.

   Are you going to ______ *with us?*

9. Rewrite the two words that need capital letters.

   yesterday, i visited my grandmother.

10. Write the missing verb.
    talk ***speak*** ***describe***

    Can you please ______ *what you saw?*

11. Circle the adjective.

    Pat's brother has a new puppy; it is called Axel.

12. Write the adjective in the correct form. ***light***

    My hair always gets ______ *in the summer.*

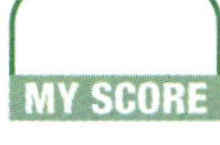

Day 2

1. What is the base word of ***farmed*** and ***farming***?

2. ***drop*** + ***ing*** =

3. Circle and rewrite the misspelt word.
   We waited for the ketle to boil, then made tea.

4. Change the verb and rewrite in the present tense.
   I ran to school.

5. Which one is not a word?
   unfair unwent undone

6. Circle the word that rhymes with ***bread***.
   skid died said

7. Circle the correct word.
   I'm cheering four/for the red team to win.

8. Circle the missing word.
   has have having
   Mum and I _____ to go shopping this afternoon.

9. Punctuate. **?** or **.**
   Tomorrow is Friday

10. Circle the tense this sentence is written in. ***past present future***
    Jack eats lunch with his friends.

11. Circle the adjective.
    The tiny baby cried noisily.

12. Circle the missing adjective.
    younger older
    My _____ sister was born four years after me.

Day 3

1. What is the base word of ***kicked*** and ***kicking***?

2. ***hurry*** + ***ed*** =

3. Write the jumbled word correctly.
   My birthday tapry was last weekend.

4. Write the past tense form of ***say***.

5. Which one is not a word?
   fighted stepped slapped

6. Circle the rhyming words.
   ticket packet cricket

7. ***hour*** or ***our***?
   We saw all of _____ family.

8. Use ***come*** or ***coming*** in the sentence.
   Did your grandfather _____ for lunch?

9. Add two capital letters.
   mr scott is my football coach.

10. Write the missing verb. ***go went***
    Tomorrow, we'll _____ to the fair.

11. Circle the adjective.
    The happy baby was smiling.

12. Write the adjective in the correct form. ***slow***
    A snail is much _____ than an ant.

WEEK 5

Day 4

1. What is the base word of ***answered*** and ***answering***?

2. ***dad*** + ***y*** =

3. Add the word with the correct spelling. ***croud*** ***crowd***

   There was a big ______ at the football match.

4. Change the verb and rewrite in the past tense.

   I write neatly.

5. Which one is not a word?

   unlock unhook unburn

6. Circle the word that rhymes with ***heart***.

   court start heard

7. Circle the correct word.

   Our team has to bye/buy/by new jerseys.

8. Circle the missing word.
   has ***have*** ***having***

   We are ______ a party next week.

9. Punctuate. ***?*** or ***!***

   Eat your breakfast

10. Circle the tense this sentence is written in. ***past*** ***present*** ***future***

    Last week, we went to the zoo. It was great!

11. Circle the adjective.

    The skilful player joined the team.

12. Circle the missing adjective.
    tall ***shorter***

    A mouse is ______ than a giraffe.

MY SCORE

Day 5

1. What is the base word of ***shouted*** and ***shouting***?

2. ***come*** + ***ing*** =

3. Circle and rewrite the misspelt word.

   What's for dinner tonite, Mum?

4. Circle a present tense form of ***ate***.

   eated eat ated

5. Which one is not a word?

   carrying happying hurrying

6. Circle the rhyming words.

   meeting cheating patting

7. ***flower*** or ***flour***?

   When we made bread we used ______.

8. Use ***come*** or ***coming***.

   Will you ______ to my birthday party?

9. Rewrite the two proper nouns with capital letters.

   My friend's name is ben tan.

10. Write the missing verb.
    watch ***watches***

    Mum says I ______ too much TV.

11. Circle the adjective.

    An apple is crunchy.

12. Write the adjective in the correct form. ***great***

    That performance was the ______ I've seen!

MY SCORE

Contractions

Some words can be joined together to make a new, shorter word. These are known as **contractions**.

One or more letters can be removed and replaced by a mark called an **apostrophe**. An apostrophe looks like this:

Shortening words makes them quicker and easier to say:

it + is = it's — they + are = they're

you + are = you're — we + are = we're

Some shortened words sound the same as other words:

its and it's — there, their and they're

your and you're — where, were and we're

But remember, if it has an apostrophe, it is a shortened word.

Practice questions

1. Make a contraction (shortened word).

   they are [ ]

2. Which word? ***your*** ***you're***

   Tell me the reason [ ] late.

---

1. Make a contraction (shortened word).

   we are [ ]

2. Which word? ***there*** ***their*** ***they're***

   Dad said [ ] coming home.

3. Rewrite the misspelt word correctly.

   The ruler is a meeter long. [ ]

4. What is the correct spelling for ***love*** + ***ing***? [ ]

5. Add two letters to ***happy*** to make it the opposite.

   That bear looked [ ] happy in its cage.

6. Which word can be added to make a new word? ***yellow*** ***pop***

   [ ] corn

7. Add the words ***break*** and ***brake*** in the correct places.

   Use the [ ] on your bike so you don't crash and [ ] something!

8. ***is*** or ***are***?

   He [ ] a good surfer.

9. Punctuate.

   I didn't finish my tea today [ ]

10. Question [ ] or command [ ]?

    Look at that huge bug!

11. Change the verb to past tense.

    score [ ]

12. Circle the two adjectives.

    It was sunny and warm on Sunday.

WEEK 6

Day 2

1. Make a shortened word.

   he is [ ]

2. ***Your*** or ***You're***?

   [ ] *invited to my party.*

3. Write the jumbled word correctly.

   We saw the beehives and tasted the nohye. [ ]

4. Circle the plural form of ***fence***.

   fencs fences fencies

5. Circle three words that can be built from ***hope***.

   hoped hopeless unhope hopeful

6. Which word is NOT an opposite of ***warm***?

   cool hot cold

7. Add two letters to make a word that means made ***cold***.

   The drinks [ ] *illed in the fridge.*

8. ***has*** or ***have***?

   She [ ] *a nice house.*

9. Circle the word that needs a capital letter.

   tomorrow thailand yesterday

10. Circle two nouns.

    The puppy played happily in the garden.

11. Circle the tense this sentence is written in. ***past present future***

    They saw that film last week.

12. Change the ending to make this word mean the ***most long***.

    longer [ ]

MY SCORE

Day 3

1. Make a shortened word.

   she is [ ]

2. Which word? ***there their they're***

   There are two cars over [ ].

3. Write the jumbled word correctly.

   Autumn is my favourite easnos. [ ]

4. What is the correct spelling for ***wed*** + ***ing***? [ ]

5. Add two letters to ***lock*** to make it the opposite.

   Can you [ ] *lock the door so we can get in?*

6. Which word can be added to make a new word? ***one side***

   some [ ]

7. Circle the correct word. ***dear deer***

   The _____ ran swiftly through the forest.

8. ***was*** or ***were***?

   My grandad [ ] *a soldier in the war.*

9. Punctuate.

   When is the next bus coming

10. Question [ ] or statement [ ]?

    What's the time?

11. Change this verb to make it present tense.

    threw [ ]

12. Circle the adjective.

    Jane's book was heavy.

MY SCORE

Day 4

1. Make a shortened word.

   I am [ ]

2. ***your*** or ***you're***?

   What's [ ] name?

3. Add the word with the correct spelling. ***amownt*** ***amount***

   Make sure you pay the right [ ] of money.

4. Circle the singular form of ***keys***.

   key keies

5. Circle two words that can be built from ***help***.

   helpness helping helpful helpy

6. Which word is NOT an opposite of ***begin***?

   start end finish

7. Add two letters to make a word that means ***sparkle and flash***.

   My kite [ ]immers in the sun.

8. ***is*** or ***are***?

   Tomorrow we [ ] going to the park.

9. Circle the word that needs a capital letter.

   june winter sister

10. Circle two nouns.

    The terrifying snake slithered through the tall grass.

11. Circle the tense this sentence is written in. ***past*** ***present*** ***future***

    We had pizza for dinner last night.

12. Change the ending to make this word mean the ***most busy***.

    busier [ ]

MY SCORE

Day 5

1. Make a shortened word.

   that is [ ]

2. ***There***, ***Their*** or ***They're***?

   [ ] going to drop me off after training.

3. Add the word with the correct spelling. ***busyly*** ***busily***

   The children worked [ ] on their projects.

4. What is the correct spelling for ***carry*** + ***ed***? [ ]

5. Add two letters to ***safe*** to make it the opposite.

   The children were being [ ]safe near the road.

6. Which word can be added to make a new word? ***my*** ***you***

   [ ]self

7. Add the words ***here*** and ***hear*** in the correct places.

   Did you [ ] the news? Your favourite band is playing [ ] next month.

8. ***has*** or ***have***?

   We [ ] to leave early.

9. Punctuate.

   Red is my favourite colour

10. Command [ ] or statement [ ]?

    I am not going to school tomorrow.

11. Change the verb to past tense.

    catch [ ]

12. Circle two adjectives.

    The soup is hot and tasty!

MY SCORE

WEEK 7

Skill focus

Alphabetical order

Knowing **alphabetical order** is an important skill. It helps you find words in the dictionary.

Putting words in order is easy when their first letters are different.

The word that starts with the letter that comes first in the alphabet goes first, the next word starts with the next letter, and so on.

bird *cat* *dog* *fish* *mouse*

When all the words start with the same letter, use the second letter instead to help you put them in order.

paint *pencil* *poster*

Practice questions

1. Number the words in alphabetical order.

   talk ☐ shout ☐ whisper ☐

2. Is this order correct?

   yes ☐ no ☐

   flower grass tree

Day 1

1. Number the words in alphabetical order.

   run ☐ play ☐ jump ☐

2. Is this order correct? yes ☐ no ☐

   crawl hop walk

3. Spell the word correctly.

   I washt my hair. ☐

4. Circle the correct spelling of ***swim*** + ***ing***.

   swiming swimming

5. ***I'm*** means:

   I am ☐ I will ☐

6. ***your*** or ***you're***?

   When is ☐ *birthday?*

7. Circle the opposites.

   laugh giggle cry

8. ***has***, ***have*** or ***having***?

   I ☐ *an older brother and a younger sister.*

9. Add the missing apostrophe. (')

   Do you think shes going to be late?

10. Circle two proper nouns.

    James was born in Adelaide.

11. Add the correct form of ***care*** to the sentence.

    My sister ☐ *about animals a lot.*

12. Circle the missing adjective.

    friendly ***shiny***

    My brother's car is black and _____.

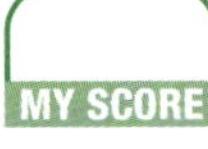

WEEK 7

Day 2

1. Number the words in alphabetical order.

   apple ☐ pear ☐ banana ☐

2. Is this order correct? yes ☐ no ☐

   orange pineapple cherry

3. Circle and rewrite the misspelt word.

   Jane is my closest frend. ☐

4. What is the base word of ***copied*** and ***copying***? ☐

5. ***That's*** means:

   that is ☐ that will ☐

6. Add two letters to make a word that means ***air coming in and out of lungs***.

   I took a deep brea☐ before I dived under.

7. Which word means the ***middle***?

   bore core

8. ***its*** or ***it's***?

   My dog hurt ☐ paw.

9. This sentence is a question ☐ or a statement ☐?

   Will it rain tomorrow?

10. Circle two nouns.

    My cat likes to eat fish.

11. Finish the pattern.

    I slice. You slice.

    He ☐.

12. Circle the adjective.

    The tree is enormous!

MY SCORE

Day 3

1. Circle the next word in alphabetical order.

   because behave began behind

2. Is this order correct? yes ☐ no ☐

   tea water coffee

3. Circle and rewrite the jumbled word.

   Be careful lifting that box, it's very vhyea. ☐

4. Circle the correct spelling of ***happy*** + ***ness***.

   happiness happyness

5. ***It's*** can mean:

   it is ☐ it will ☐

6. ***Your*** or ***You're***?

   ☐ *really funny!*

7. Which word is NOT an opposite of ***full***?

   hungry over empty

8. ***was*** or ***were***?

   She ☐ a good singer.

9. Add the missing apostrophe. (')

   Im so surprised to see you here!

10. Circle the proper noun in the sentence.

    In June, our class is going to the zoo.

11. Add the correct form of ***eat*** to the sentence.

    We ☐ lunch.

12. Circle the missing adjective.

    black new dull

    Sam's _____ bike is red and shiny.

MY SCORE

Day 4

1. Write in alphabetical order.

again any after

2. Is this order correct? yes no

skin spin swim

3. Add the word with the correct spelling. ***Febuary February***

My birthday is in ____.

4. What is the base word of ***said*** and ***saying***? ____

5. ***He's*** can mean:

he is he will

6. Add two letters to make a word that means ***after third***.

I came four____ in the race.

7. Which word means ***not smooth***?

rough tough

8. ***its*** or ***it's***?

Time for bed kids, ____ late!

9. This sentence is a question or a statement ?

I like apples and bananas.

10. Circle two nouns.

The bottle was on the table.

11. Finish the pattern.

I paint. You paint.

He ____.

12. Circle the adjective.

Jan's house is huge!

MY SCORE

Day 5

1. Number the words in alphabetical order.

comb crumb calm

2. Is this order correct? yes no

peach pink purple

3. Add the word with the correct spelling. ***rong wrong***

I took the ____ book.

4. Circle the correct spelling of ***care*** + ***ing***.

careing caring

5. ***She's*** can mean:

she is she will

6. ***your*** or ***you're***?

Where are ____ shoes?

7. Circle the opposites.

come go run

8. ***has***, ***have*** or ***having***?

Jamie ____ a party on Sunday.

9. Add the missing apostrophe. (')

Can you tell me whats wrong?

10. Circle the proper nouns.

I live at number 37 on Westburn Road.

11. Add the correct form of ***write*** to the sentence.

My friend ____ me emails every week.

12. Circle the missing adjective.

kind mean

Mrs James is a ____ and caring teacher.

MY SCORE

WEEK 8

Day 1

1. Circle and rewrite the misspelt word.
   Can I ride that bike insted?
2. Number the words in alphabetical order.
   doesn't ☐ dancer ☐ didn't ☐
3. Circle the words that make the shortened word ***I'm***.
   I is   I can   I am
4. Add two letters to ***invited*** to make the opposite.
   I was ☐ invited to her party after we had an argument.
5. What is the correct spelling for ***lift*** + ***ing***? ☐
6. ***seen*** or ***saw***?
   I ☐ your cat on my driveway.
7. ***your*** or ***you're***?
   Did you bring ☐ lunch?
8. Punctuate.
   Let me know when youre ready to go.
9. Circle the past tense form of ***cry***.
   cryed   cried   cries
10. Circle the proper noun.
    Gemma is my best friend.
11. Circle the tense this sentence is written in. ***past*** ***present*** ***future***
    Our class went on an excursion to the zoo.
12. Circle the two adjectives.
    I wore a green shirt and blue shoes.

MY SCORE

Day 2

1. Circle and rewrite the misspelt word.
   The twin boys ran ahed of their sister. ☐
2. Circle the next word in alphabetical order.
   ghost   garden   grapes   gift
3. Circle the letter left out to make the shortened word ***I'm***.
   u   e   a
4. Add two letters to make the opposite.
   ☐ opened
5. Add ***under*** to make a new word.
   break   ground ☐
6. ***is*** or ***are***?
   Mr Jones ☐ my neighbour.
7. Circle the correct word. ***cell*** ***sell***
   Mum and Dad are trying to _____ our house.
8. Add capital letters.
   my favourite day is christmas day.
9. Write the past tense form of ***wait***. ☐
10. Write the missing noun.
    books ***paper***
    Karen is always reading ☐.
11. Circle the verb.
    I scored four goals in the match.
12. Change the ending to make this word mean the ***most full***.
    fuller ☐

WEEK 8

Day 3

1. Circle and rewrite the misspelt word.

   Please don't showt at me! [ ]

2. Write in alphabetical order.

   swore shore store

   [ ] [ ] [ ]

3. Circle the words that make the shortened word ***I've***.

   I of I have I am

4. Add two letters to ***clean*** to make the opposite.

   Our hotel was [ ]clean.

5. Circle the correct spelling ***thin*** + ***ing***.

   thining thinning

6. ***was*** or ***were***?

   Last year, we [ ] in Bali for Christmas.

7. ***there***, ***their*** or ***they're***?

   Can you see the ball over [ ] in the grass?

8. Punctuate.

   Dad said hes going to be late.

9. Write the missing verb. ***play plays***

   Jed [ ] the guitar and the drums.

10. Circle the proper noun.

    I like Fridays best.

11. Circle the tense this sentence is written in. ***past present future***

    The yellow team won the school trophy.

12. Circle the adjective.

    The TV show on yesterday was funny.

    MY SCORE

Day 4

1. Circle and rewrite the misspelt word.

   Can you lend me your pensil? [ ]

2. Circle the next word in alphabetical order.

   taught touch teach taste

3. Circle the letters left out to make the shortened word ***I've***.

   ha do wi

4. Add two letters to make the opposite.

   [ ]zipped

5. Which one is not a word?

   supermarket superstar supermouse

6. ***seen*** or ***saw***?

   I've never [ ] snow.

7. Circle the correct word. ***bury berry***

   I watched the dog _____ its bone.

8. Add capital letters.

   i made a card for valentine's day.

9. Write a present tense form of ***shouted***. [ ]

10. Write the missing noun. ***jeans jumper***

    I went shopping and bought a new [ ].

11. Circle the verb.

    Anna shut the small window.

12. Change the ending to make this word mean the ***most straight***.

    straighter [ ]

    MY SCORE

Day 5

1. Circle and rewrite the misspelt word.

   I drew a hart shape and coloured it in red. [ ]

2. Number the words in alphabetical order.

   eleven [ ] eight [ ] enemy [ ]

3. Circle the words that make the shortened word ***that's***.

   that is what is

4. Add two letters to ***prepared*** to make the opposite.

   I was [ ] prepared for the big test.

5. What is the correct spelling for ***carry*** + ***ing***? [ ]

6. ***is*** or ***are***?

   You [ ] very late!

7. ***your*** or ***you're***?

   When [ ] ready, we can go.

8. Punctuate.

   Do you think theyre home

9. Circle a present tense form of ***sat***.

   sitted sitter sit

10. Circle the proper noun.

    Laura likes swimming.

11. Circle the tense this sentence is written in. ***past present future***

    Miss Jones sings in the choir.

12. Circle two adjectives.

    The old computer needs a modern mouse.

Skill focus review

WEEK 8

1. Circle and rewrite the misspelt word.

   At the circus the clowns made me laff a lot. [ ]

2. Write in alphabetical order.

   red rash ring

   [ ] [ ] [ ]

3. Which words make ***I've***?

   I am I have I will

4. ***thin*** + ***er*** = [ ]

5. Add the words ***they're*** and ***their*** in the correct places.

   [ ] *coming to show us* [ ] *car.*

6. Punctuate. ***?*** or ***!***

   Where are you going [ ]

7. This sentence is a command [ ] or a question [ ]?

   Did you feed the dog?

8. Circle the noun.

   My blue blanket is very warm.

9. Circle the proper noun.

   make she James

10. Circle the verb.

    We swim at the beach often.

11. Circle the tense this sentence is written in. ***past present future***

    She stepped on broken glass.

12. Circle the missing adjective. ***dangerous hairy***

    The _____ snake was in the grass.

WEEK 9

Skill focus

Who does it belong to?

To show that something belongs to someone or something, a small mark and ***s*** is added to the end of the word.

The small mark we use is called an **apostrophe**.

The tail of the apostrophe points to the owner.

We usually do not need to change the word before adding the apostrophe and ***s***.

Remember!

An apostrophe is only used when we want to show that something belongs to someone or something.

We never add apostrophes to plural nouns:

✓ two bananas ✗ ~~two banana's~~

Practice questions

1. The desk belongs to ______.
   The child's desk was very messy.

2. Write the missing word.
   Helens ***Helen's***
   I like ______ drawing the most.

Day 1

1. The dog belongs to ______.
   Jack's dog, Fred, loves to play fetch.

2. Write the missing word.
   Sams ***Sam's***
   I went in ______ car.

3. Circle and rewrite the misspelt word.
   Do you know were the canteen is? ______

4. Number the words in alphabetical order.
   poison ☐ person ☐ people ☐

5. Circle the correct shortened word.
   I'll i'll

6. Add two letters to make this word mean the opposite.
   ☐sure

7. Circle the correct spelling ***move*** + ***ing***.
   moving moveing

8. The opposite of ***left*** is ______.

9. ***your*** or ***you're***?
   How is ______ mum?

10. Add four capital letters.
    simon and anna went to south africa.

11. Statement ☐ or question ☐?
    What is you favourite colour?

12. Circle the better noun.
    horse ***bird***
    The _____ galloped through the paddock.

Day 2

1. The dress belongs to [ ].
   The girl's dress was long and silky.
2. Write the missing word.
   John's ***Johns***
   Did you see [ ] house?
3. Circle and rewrite the misspelt word.
   The childrn played in the garden. [ ]
4. Write in alphabetical order.
   south soap sound
   [ ] [ ] [ ]
5. Which letters are left out of ***I'll***?
   ha wi no
6. Add two letters to make this word mean the opposite.
   [ ]kind
7. ***mum*** + ***y*** = [ ]
8. Circle the word closest in meaning to ***evening***.
   night morning day
9. ***to***, ***too*** or ***two***?
   Did you go [ ] the park?
10. Add punctuation to the end of the sentence.
    Next week is the start of the football season[ ]
11. This sentence is a command [ ] or a question [ ]?
    Get your shoes off the table!
12. Circle the proper noun.
    I spoke to Mike on the phone.

MY SCORE

Day 3

1. The ball belongs to [ ].
   We played with Jenna's ball at lunchtime.
2. Write the missing word. ***dogs*** ***dog's***
   There were four [ ] at the park.
3. Write the jumbled word correctly.
   I like to twach my sister play basketball. [ ]
4. Write in alphabetical order.
   heart heavy head
   [ ] [ ] [ ]
5. Circle the words that make the shortened word ***what's***.
   it is what is
6. Make a new word. ***pre*** ***post***
   *Hint: **pre** means **before**; **post** means **after**.*
   [ ]view
7. Circle the correct spelling of ***skip*** + ***ing***.
   skipping skiping
8. The opposite of ***up*** is [ ].
9. Which word? ***there*** ***their*** ***they're***
   Do you think ___ still coming?
10. Add three capital letters.
    next week, i'll see my friend peter.
11. Statement [ ] or question [ ]?
    How much is that cupcake?
12. Circle the better noun.
    man ***woman***
    My granny is a friendly ___.

MY SCORE

WEEK 9

Day 4

1. The playground belongs to ______.
   My school's playground is fun to play on.
2. Write the missing word. ***Jims*** ***Jim's***
   I saw ______ new bike.
3. Add the word with the correct spelling. ***strate*** ***straight***
   Draw a ______ line on your paper.
4. Circle the last word in alphabetical order.
   chain cheese chips cheek
5. Circle the correct word. ***youl'l*** ***you'll***
6. Make a new word. ***pre*** ***post***
   ______made
7. ***spine*** + ***y*** = ______
8. Circle the word closest in meaning to ***disappear***.
   found vanish control
9. ***by***, ***bye*** or ***buy***?
   What did you ______ for me?
10. Add punctuation to the end of the sentence.
    Where did you go today ☐
11. This sentence is a command ☐ or a question ☐?
    Tell your sister it's time for dinner.
12. Circle two proper nouns.
    I would like to visit India and China.

MY SCORE

Day 5

1. The DVD belongs to ______.
   We watched Kim's DVD after lunch.
2. Write the missing word.
   Jenny's ***Jennys***
   That is ______ lunch box.
3. Circle and rewrite the misspelt word.
   Try not to brak your new toy. ______
4. Write in alphabetical order.
   parcel parent pardon
   ______ ______ ______
5. Which letters are left out of ***you'll***?
   wi ha no
6. Make a new word. ***pre*** ***post***
   ______caution
7. Circle the correct spelling of ***know*** + ***ing***. *Hint:* ***ow*** *makes a* ***long o*** *sound.*
   knowwing knowing
8. The opposite of ***then*** is ______.
9. ***your*** or ***you're***?
   I think ______ right!
10. Add four capital letters.
    the opera house is a famous landmark in sydney.
11. Statement ☐ or question ☐?
    I went for a walk through the forest.
12. Circle the better noun. ***car*** ***bus***
    The large group of children boarded the ____.

MY SCORE

Skill focus

Verb groups and tense

Verbs are words that show an action like *run, jump* or *play*.

Verbs can also tell us about being or having.

The verbs ***to be*** and ***to have*** have many forms.

Their form depends on the **tense**.

It also depends on the person or people that are doing the action.

to be

Past tense:	was	were	
Present tense:	am	are	is
Future tense:	will be		

to have

Past tense:	had	
Present tense:	have	has
Future tense:	will have	

These words are often used to make verbs with more than one part. They are called verb groups.

The children ***are going*** *on an excursion today.*
verb group

Verb groups and the endings of verbs work together to tell us when something happens.

Practice questions

1. Circle the verb group.
   My little brother is starting school on Monday.
2. Circle the missing word.
   is ***am*** ***are***
   We ___ going to be late for school.

Day 1

WEEK 10

1. Circle the verb group.
   Lee was fishing from the riverbank.
2. ***was*** or ***were***?
   Jo and Ida [ ] *laughing.*
3. Rewrite the misspelt word correctly.
   We woke up erly today. [ ]
4. Number the words in alphabetical order.
   least [ ] learnt [ ] latch [ ]
5. Circle the missing word.
   Who's ***What's***
   *Hint: '**s** can mean has, is or was.*
   ___ happening at the school fair?
6. ***quick*** + ***ly*** = [ ]
7. Which word means ***below***?
   under over
8. Circle the correct word.
   My shoe had a whole/hole in it.
9. Add the missing apostrophe. (')
   Dan and Jills dog is black and white.
10. Add four capital letters.
    i live on the corner of green and brown street.
11. Circle two nouns.
    My phone is in my bag.
12. Circle the correct adjective.
    brighter ***brightest***
    Sirius is ___ than all the other stars.

WEEK 10

Day 2

1. Circle the verb group.

   Casey is going home now.

2. ***is***, ***am*** or ***are***?

   I ☐ *cooking a big feast for dinner.*

3. Write the jumbled word correctly.

   I wish I could see into the tufure. ☐

4. Circle the word you can add to ***noon***.

   before   after

5. Which shortened word goes in the box? ***who's*** ***what's***

   My aunt, ☐ *a singer, was on the news.*

6. ***sick*** + ***ly*** = ☐

7. Circle the opposite of ***above***.

   below   near   through

8. ***seen*** or ***saw***?

   I've already ☐ *that film.*

9. Circle the missing word. ***cat's cats***

   My next-door neighbour has ten ____.

10. Add four capital letters.

    saint patrick's day is in march.

11. Circle the proper noun in the sentence.

    My birthday is in May and so is my dad's.

12. Write the adjective. ☐

    The small mouse scampered under the fence.

MY SCORE

Day 3

1. Circle the verb group.

   James was eating a peach.

2. ***was*** or ***were***?

   Jim ☐ *sick last night.*

3. Write the jumbled word correctly.

   Kim saw a somufa TV star in the city. ☐

4. Number the words in alphabetical order.

   white ☐ which ☐ where ☐

5. Write the missing word.
   Who's ***What's***

   '☐ *happening over there?' Mum asked.*

6. ***slow*** + ***ly*** = ☐

7. Circle the word closest in meaning to ***modern***.

   new   ancient   visible

8. Circle the correct word.

   I need to get out of the son/sun; it's too hot!

9. Add the missing apostrophe. (')

   My dads favourite meal is spaghetti and meatballs.

10. Add two capital letters.

    pizza comes from italy.

11. Circle three nouns.

    Amy opened the tin before dinner.

12. Circle the correct adjective.
    dirtier ***dirtiest***

    Our car was the ____ in the car park.

MY SCORE

Day 4

1. Circle the verb group.

   We are going to Spain.

2. ***is***, ***am*** or ***are***?

   We [ ] *going on holiday to Brazil.*

3. Add the word with the correct spelling. ***Thailand*** ***Tiland***

   My aunt lives in [ ].

4. Circle the word you can add to ***mark***.

   page book

5. Which shortened word goes in the box? ***who's*** ***what's***

   That man, [ ] *over there, is selling tickets.*

6. ***cry*** + ***ing*** = [ ]

   *Hint: keep **y** when you add **ing**.*

7. Circle the opposite of ***dull***.

   hard flat bright

8. ***seen*** or ***saw***?

   I [ ] *a tiger at the zoo.*

9. Circle the missing word. ***cat's cats***

   My _____ name is Mittens.

10. Add capital letters.

    my mum and i like to read harry potter books.

11. Circle the proper nouns in the sentence.

    Liam has lived in Cape Town and Durban.

12. Write the adjective. [ ]

    Harry stared at his broken toys.

Day 5

1. Circle the verb group.

   We are learning the drums in our music class.

2. ***was*** or ***were***?

   We [ ] *baking a cake.*

3. Add the word with the correct spelling. ***afraid*** ***afrad***

   I am [ ] *of spiders.*

4. Write in alphabetical order.

   quote quiz quake

   [ ] [ ] [ ]

5. Circle the missing word.
   Who's ***What's***

   '_____ been eating all the biscuits?' asked Gran.

6. ***fly*** + ***ing*** = [ ]

7. Which word means ***quick*** or ***fast***?

   swift lift

8. Circle the correct word.

   Jo went on the roller-coaster at the fare/fair.

9. Add the missing apostrophe. (')

   I am going to Jennys house after school.

10. Add capital letters.

    this thursday, mr rowe is taking his class to the museum in perth.

11. Circle two nouns.

    Lions live in Africa.

12. Circle the correct adjective.
    older ***oldest***

    I am _____ than my little brother.

WEEK 10

Skill focus

Rules for making plural nouns

If we want to show that we have more than one person, place or thing, we usually add an **s** or **es** (words ending in **ch**, **sh**, **s**, **x** or **z**).

When this happens, the base word does not change:

*one **lion***

*a group of **lion<u>s</u>***

*one **fox***

*a family of **fox<u>es</u>***

However, some nouns don't follow this rule:

- When a noun ends with a consonant then ***y***, we change the ***y*** to an ***i*** and add ***es*** to make a plural.

  Change the ***y*** to ***i*** and add ***es***:

  i
  pupp~~y~~es = puppies

- When a noun ends in ***f***, we change the ***f*** to ***v*** and add ***es*** to make a plural.

  Change the ***f*** to ***v*** and add ***es***:

  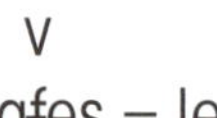

  v
  lea~~f~~es = leaves

- There are even some nouns that become a different word when they are plural:

one <u>mouse</u>

lots of <u>mice</u>

Practice questions

1. Circle the plural form of ***wolf***.

   wolves wolfs wolfes

2. Circle the singular form of ***babies***.

   babie baby babye

Day 1

1. Circle the plural form of ***wife***.

   women wives wifes

2. Circle the singular form of ***berries***.

   berry berrie

3. Rewrite the misspelt word correctly.

   We have to way the ingredients for the cake. [ ]

4. ***They've*** means [ ].

5. Add two letters to make this word mean the opposite.

   [ ]even

6. Which word is the opposite of ***loud***?

   quite quiet

7. Circle two rhyming words.

   dance fence chance

8. Circle the missing word.
   Sarahs ***Sarah's***

   What is _____ address?

9. ***your*** or ***you're***?

   May I borrow [ ] *pen?*

10. Circle the tense this sentence is written in. ***past*** ***present*** ***future***

    Sam and Tim will watch the final this weekend.

11. Circle the verb and rewrite in the present tense.

    At school, we made cards for our parents.

    [ ]

12. Circle the missing word.
    brought ***bought***
    Hint: buy=bought; bring=brought

    We _____ a new car last week.

WEEK 11

Day 2

1. Circle the plural form of ***strawberry***.

strawberryes strawberrys strawberries

2. Circle the singular form of ***calves***.

calv calf

3. Circle and rewrite the misspelt word.

My parents are bying me a new bike.

4. ***We've*** means ______.

5. Add ***ly*** to make a new word.

sad fast ______

6. Circle the word closest in meaning to ***wealth***.

information surprise riches

7. ***bare*** or ***bear***?

The grizzly ______ wandered slowly through the woods.

8. Punctuate. ***?*** or ***!***

Help, fire ___

9. ***it's*** or ***its***?

My bike lost ______ chain yesterday.

10. Circle the tense this sentence is written in. ***past present future***

I am going to the park now.

11. ***was*** or ***were***?

Jay's friends ______ playing in the park.

12. ***go***, ***goes*** or ***gone***?

That bus ______ past every morning.

MY SCORE

Day 3

1. Circle the plural of ***man***.

man mans men

2. Circle the singular form of ***teeth***.

tooths tooth teeths

3. Circle and rewrite the jumbled word.

The farm grows heatw and corn. ______

4. Write in alphabetical order.

shell spell smell

______ ______ ______

5. Add two letters to make this word mean the opposite.

___tested

6. Circle the opposite of ***odd***.

even strange number

7. Circle two rhyming words.

they then those stay

8. Circle the missing word.

Jennifer's Jennifers

Use _____ computer.

9. Circle the missing word.

there their they're

Can they bring _____ chairs?

10. Circle the tense this sentence is written in. ***past present future***

Mum will make cupcakes for my birthday in May.

11. Circle the verb and rewrite in the present tense.

We watched the game.

______

12. Which word? ***brought bought***

Sania _____ a salad to the picnic.

MY SCORE

WEEK 11

Day 4

1. Circle the plural form of ***elf***.
   elves elfs elfes
2. Circle the singular form of ***batteries***.
   battery batterie battere
3. Add the word with the correct spelling. ***Wensday Wednesday***
   We visit the library every ______.
4. ***They'll*** means ______.
5. Add ***ly*** to make a new word.
   rough eat ______
6. Circle the word closest in meaning to ***drink***.
   pour spill sip
7. ***four*** or ***for***?
   Are you ready ______ *school?*
8. Punctuate. ***?*** or ***.***
   Don't forget your bag ___
9. ***its*** or ***it's***?
   Turn on your headlights when ______ *dark.*
10. Circle the tense this sentence is written in. ***past present future***
    Dad was singing loudly in the shower.
11. ***is*** or ***are***?
    Where ______ *the dog's bowl?*
12. ***go***, ***goes*** or ***gone***?
    Where did the cat ______*?*

MY SCORE

Day 5

1. Circle the plural form of ***thief***.
   thiefs thieves thiefes
2. Circle the singular form of ***selves***.
   self selve selv
3. Add the word with the correct spelling. ***stopped stoped***
   The car ______ *suddenly.*
4. ***We'll*** means ______.
5. Add two letters to make this word mean the opposite.
   ___done
6. Circle the opposite of ***fake***.
   story real pretend
7. Circle the rhyming words.
   should shall stood
8. Circle the missing word.
   Jans Jan's
   ______ *hair is straight.*
9. ***your*** or ***you're***?
   Where is ______ *ruler?*
10. Circle the tense this sentence is written in. ***past present future***
    We will take the dog for a walk this afternoon.
11. Circle the verb and rewrite in the present tense.
    I studied hard for my test.
    ______
12. Which word? ***brought bought***
    I ______ *my rugby ball to school.*

MY SCORE

Skill focus

Why do we add *re-* and *sub-* to words?

Sometimes, groups of letters are added to the beginning of words.

This makes a new word which has a different meaning from the **base word**.

A **base word** is a word that doesn't have any word parts added to it.

The word part ***re*** is usually added to a verb. It means to ***do again***.

write → rewrite

build → rebuild

The word part ***sub*** means ***under*** or ***below***.

marine (sea) → submarine (under sea)

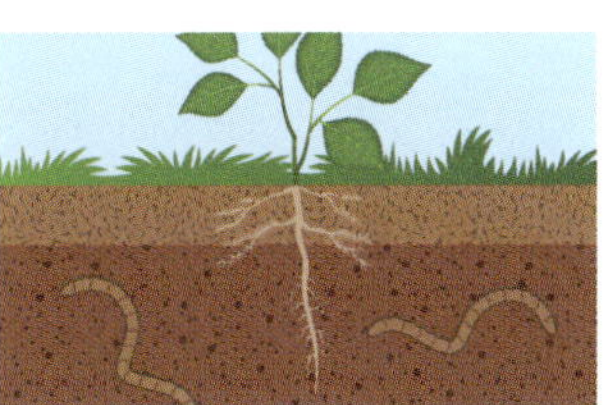

soil → subsoil (soil below)

Practice questions

1. Which one of these can be added to make a new word? ***sub*** ***re***

play

2. Which one is not a word?

rewind retie recry

Day 1

1. Which one of these can be added to make a new word? ***sub*** ***re***

   [ ]do

2. Which one is not a word?

   submerge subway subfix

3. Add the word with the correct spelling. ***height*** ***hite***

   The cat jumped from a great [ ].

4. Circle the plural of ***child***.

   children childs

5. Add ***ful*** to make a new word.

   play good [ ]

6. Circle the opposite of ***true***.

   false real fact

7. Which word means ***fog***?

   mist missed

8. ***chews*** or ***choose***?

   Dad asked me to [ ] *a cake for dessert.*

9. Circle the word that needs a capital letter.

   forgotten mexico metre

10. Add capital letters.

    everybody likes to celebrate on new year's eve.

11. ***your*** or ***you're***?

    Now it's [ ] *turn.*

12. Use ***laugh*** or ***laughs*** in the sentence.

    My sister [ ] *like a hyena!*

WEEK 12

Day 2

1. Which one of these can be added to make a new word? ***sub*** ***re***

   [ ]merge

2. Which one is not a word?

   remind rehappy review

3. Add the word with the correct spelling. ***erthquake*** ***earthquake***

   The [ ] made the ground shake.

4. Circle the plural of ***knife***.

   knives knifes

5. Which one of these can be added to make a new word? ***sub*** ***re*** ***un***

   [ ]lucky

6. Circle the opposites.

   funny boring smile

7. Which word is NOT the opposite of ***open***?

   touch close shut

8. Circle two rhyming words.

   wait cut straight puppet

9. Punctuate.

   I'm sorry, I forgot my homework

10. This sentence is a command [ ], question [ ] or statement [ ].

    What time does it start?

11. ***was*** or ***were***?

    We [ ] looking for you.

12. Write the missing noun.
    bedroom ***phone***

    I spoke to Jessica on the [ ].

MY SCORE

Day 3

1. Which one of these can be added to make a new word? ***sub*** ***re***

   [ ]act

2. Which one is not a word?

   subplay submit submarine

3. Add the word with the correct spelling. ***weke*** ***weak***

   The ill boy was [ ].

4. Circle the plural form of ***tooth***.

   toothes teeth

5. Add ***ness*** to make a new word.

   sad friend [ ]

6. Which word does NOT have a similar meaning to ***cool***?

   cold steamy chilly

7. Which word has a similar meaning to ***story***?

   tail tale

8. ***meat*** or ***meet***?

   What time would you like to [ ]?

9. Circle the word that needs a capital letter.

   march might must

10. Add capital letters.

    athens is the capital city of greece.

11. ***your*** or ***you're***?

    Hurry up, [ ] late!

12. Use ***come*** or ***coming*** in the sentence.

    Are Donna and Jan [ ] too?

MY SCORE

WEEK 12

Day 4

1. Which one of these can be added to make a new word? ***sub*** ***re***

   [ ]way

2. Which one is not a word?

   replay reyoung return

3. Add the word with the correct spelling. ***quick*** ***qick***

   I had a [ ] nap before the party.

4. Circle the singular form of ***babies***.

   babie babby baby

5. Which one of these can be added to make a new word? ***sub*** ***re*** ***un***

   [ ]equal

6. Which word is the opposite of ***receive***?

   give go

7. Which word is NOT the opposite of ***ugly***?

   mean beautiful pretty

8. Circle the rhyming words.

   tray weigh gate

9. Punctuate.

   I'm happy my team won

10. This sentence is a command [ ], question [ ] or statement [ ]?

    James is shorter than Sam.

11. ***is*** or ***are***?

    The apples [ ] in the bowl.

12. Circle the missing noun. ***crab*** ***fish***

    We caught lots of ______ in our net.

MY SCORE

Day 5

1. Which one of these can be added to make a new word? ***sub*** ***re***

   [ ]count

2. Which one is not a word?

   subtitle subtract subwalk

3. Add the word with the correct spelling. ***heath*** ***health***

   Daily exercise helps you look after your [ ].

4. Circle the next word in alphabetical order.

   shadow shawl shallow shame

5. Make a new word. ***ful*** ***ness***

   cheer[ ]

6. Circle the opposite words.

   save spend shop

7. Which word has a similar meaning to ***enlarged***?

   grown groan

8. ***hour*** or ***our***?

   We had to wait for an [ ].

9. Which words need a capital letter?

   paris january friends

10. Rewrite two words with capitals.

    adam's sister, emily, goes to university.

    [ ] [ ]

11. ***your*** or ***you're***?

    I like [ ] dress.

12. Add the correct form of ***ask***.

    Jamie [ ] me to meet him at the park.

MY SCORE

WEEK 13

Skill focus

Is not, am not, are not

Sometimes, two words can be joined together to make a shorter word:

they + have = they've   we + will = we'll

Many shortened words are made by adding the word ***not*** to another word.

When shortening two words with the word ***not***, the ***o*** is usually removed and replaced with an apostrophe between the ***n*** and the ***t***.

The first word doesn't usually change:

do + not = don't

There are two shortened words that don't follow this rule:

1. ***will not*** changes to ***won't***.
2. ***can not*** changes to ***can't***.

Adding not makes a **negative form** of the word. This makes the word it is added to not true.

She is going to the party.

She isn't doing to the party.

Practice questions

1. Circle the words that make ***haven't***.

   have not   havent not   has not

2. Add the negative form of ***must*** to the sentence.

   You [ ] leave your bike in the rain.

Day 1

1. Circle the letter left out to make the shortened word ***shouldn't***.

   a   o   i

2. Add the negative form of ***has*** to the sentence.

   Dad [ ] seen that film yet.

3. Circle and rewrite the misspelt word.

   I had to make a choyce between playing netball or basketball. [ ]

4. Add the prefix ***re*** to make a new word.

   part   build [ ]

5. Make a new word. ***ful*** ***ness***

   thank[ ]

6. Write the plural form of ***foot***.

   [ ]

7. Which word can be added to ***skate***?

   board   boy

8. Circle two words close in meaning.

   wept   smiled   cried

9. Is the apostrophe used correctly?

   yes [ ] no [ ]

   Please put those cup's in the sink.

10. ***seen*** or ***saw***?

    We [ ] a helicopter in the sky.

11. Circle the tense this sentence is written in. ***past*** ***present*** ***future***

    I spent all of my money at the school fair.

12. Circle the adjective.

    I read a fantastic book.

Day 2

1. Circle the words that make ***won't***.

   won not   will not

2. Add the missing apostrophe. (')

   I havent seen her new schoolbag.

3. Circle and rewrite the misspelt word.

   My mum and dad are afraid of heigts.

4. Which one of these can be added to make a new word? ***sub*** ***re***

   fresh

5. Make a new word. ***ful*** ***ness***

   happy

6. Write the plural form of ***lady***.

7. Circle the rhyming words.

   peach   catch   teach

8. Add the words ***ate*** and ***eight*** in the correct places.

   The ______ -tentacled octopus ______ the prawn.

9. Add capitals. How many?

   my friend ella loves the harry potter series by J K rowling.

10. ***is*** or ***are***?

    They ______ going out for dinner.

11. Circle the missing verb. ***heard hear***

    Did you ______ what happened to Lee?

12. Circle the missing adjective.

    heavy   ***lighter***

    My puppy is getting really ______.

Day 3

WEEK 13

1. Which letter is left out from ***wouldn't***?

   a   i   o

2. Add the negative form of ***could*** to the sentence.

   We ______ see because it was too dark.

3. Circle and rewrite the misspelt word.

   It's dangerous to swing on your chare.

4. Add the prefix ***sub*** to make a new word.

   merge

5. Make a new word. ***ful*** ***ness***

   beauty

6. Write the singular form of ***cities***.

7. Which word can be added to make a new word? ***rain*** ***tie***

   bow

8. Circle the word closest in meaning to ***captured***.

   location   imprisoned   direction

9. The bottle belongs to ______.

   The baby's bottle was empty.

10. ***was*** or ***were***?

    Steve ______ eating an apple.

11. Circle the tense this sentence is written in. ***past*** ***present*** ***future***

    Martin is going to be in the school play.

12. Circle the two adjectives.

    The graceful swan floated on the still lake.

Day 4

1. Circle the words that make ***can't***.
   can not   cant not
2. Add the missing apostrophe. (')
   I wasnt ready in time this morning.
3. Circle and rewrite the misspelt word.
   Whales, sharks and fish live in the oshun.
4. Which one of these can be added to make a new word? ***sub*** ***re***
   new
5. Add ***less*** to make a new word.
   breath
6. Write the plural form of ***wolf***.
7. Circle the rhyming words.
   skipped   slapped   slipped
8. Add the words ***piece*** and ***peace*** in the correct places.
   I ate a ______ of pie at the march for ______.
9. Add capitals. How many?
   flora visited the eiffel tower in paris, france.
10. ***is*** or ***are***?
    My friends ______ in a band.
11. Circle the missing verb. ***slices slice***
    That chef ____ onions very quickly.
12. Circle the missing adjective.
    rough   ***yellow***
    The ____ dress fitted the girl perfectly.

MY SCORE

Day 5

1. Which letter is left out from ***don't***?
   a   i   o
2. Add the negative form of ***have*** to the sentence.
   I ______ been to that beach before.
3. Write the jumbled word correctly.
   We read a story about a time chmaien at school.
4. Write in alphabetical order.
   hotel   horse   house
5. Add ***less*** to make a new word.
   word
6. Write the singular form of ***fairies***.
7. Which word can be added to ***some***?
   body   person
8. Circle two words close in meaning.
   touched   picked   chose
9. Is the apostrophe used correctly?
   yes ☐   no ☐
   I play games on my mum's phone.
10. ***seen*** or ***saw***?
    Have you ______ Alex today?
11. Circle the tense this sentence is written in. ***past*** ***present*** ***future***
    We walked two kilometres yesterday.
12. Circle the two adjectives.
    The day was wet and windy so we stayed inside.

Skill focus

Other words for people or things

I	me	it
they	them	him
her	we	us

These words can be used to replace nouns in a sentence:

<u>Mum</u> is shopping. <u>She</u> bought a new dress.

The word ***she*** is used instead of the noun ***Mum*** in this sentence.

Look at the <u>ducks</u>. <u>They</u> are swimming in the pond.

The word ***they*** is used instead of the noun ***ducks*** in this sentence.

Using other words for people and things stops you from repeating the same words.

This makes your sentences easier to read.

Practice questions

1. ***we*** or ***us***?

   Would you like to come to the shop with [ ]?

2. Which word can replace the underlined word? ***it*** ***them***

   I like watching birds; watching <u>birds</u> is very relaxing.

Day 1

1. ***I*** or ***me***?

   Come with [ ] and I'll show you my puppy.

2. Circle the missing word. ***It*** ***He***

   ____ left a book at school yesterday.

3. Add the word with the correct spelling. ***hungree*** ***hungry***

   I wasn't very [ ] after eating all that cake!

4. Which one is not a word?

   refresh   return   resay

5. Add ***less*** to make a new word. *Hint: keep the **e**.*

   care[ ]

6. Shorten ***can not***. [ ]

7. Add the negative form of ***is*** to the sentence.

   Joanne [ ] coming to school today.

8. Circle the rhyming word. ***wear***

   wore   farm   care

9. Circle the correct word. ***made*** ***maid***

   The ____ cleaned the house.

10. Circle the missing word. ***children's*** ***childrens***

    I heard the ____ laughter.

11. Circle the noun.

    We did a puzzle.

12. Circle the verb.

    The girl sang beautifully.

WEEK 14

Day 2

1. ***he*** or ***him***?

   Let ______ have a turn.

2. Which word can replace the underlined words? ***it*** ***that***

   My house is on the corner; <u>my house</u> has a red door.

3. Circle and rewrite the misspelt word.

   Let's meet at the train stashun at 5 o'clock. ______

4. Which word can be added to make a new word? ***hill*** ***stop***

   down ______

5. Add ***less*** to make a new word.

   shape ______

6. ***Haven't*** means ______.

7. Circle the words that are missing. ***must have*** ***should not*** ***are not***

   You ______ go in there.

8. Circle the word that rhymes with ***height***.

   can't kite little

9. Circle the correct word. ***horse*** ***hoarse***

   My friends and I went ______ riding.

10. Add punctuation.

    I didnt know dogs ate vegetables

11. Circle the noun.

    The phone was ringing.

12. Write the missing verb. ***sat*** ***bark***

    My dog ______ on the blanket in the car.

MY SCORE

Day 3

1. ***I*** or ***me***?

   My sister teases ______ sometimes.

2. Circle the missing word. ***she*** or ***her***

   Mum was born in China; ______ speaks Mandarin.

3. Rewrite the misspelt word correctly.

   A sqware has four sides. ______

4. Add two letters.

   Make sure you put the paper in the ______cycling bin.

5. Add ***ful*** or ***ness*** to make a new word.

   hate ______

6. Shorten ***was not***. ______

7. Add the negative form of ***were*** to the sentence.

   We ______ tired, so we stayed up late.

8. Circle two rhyming words.

   fight quite start

9. Circle the correct word. ***whole*** ***hole***

   There was a ______ in the footpath.

10. Circle the missing word. ***boys*** ***boy's***

    That ______ bike is silver and red.

11. Circle the noun.

    We went to the park.

12. Circle the verb.

    My dad is very tall.

MY SCORE

WEEK 14

Day 4

1. ***they*** or ***them***?

   When will ☐ *be home?*

2. Which word can replace the underlined word? ***she*** ***what***

   Sarah is my friend; <u>Sarah</u> likes to draw pictures.

3. Write the jumbled word correctly.

   I visited my uncle's rydia farm and tasted fresh milk. ☐

4. Which word can be added to make a new word? ***time*** ***chair***

   ☐table

5. Add ***less*** or ***ness*** to make the word.

   lonely☐

6. ***Doesn't*** means ☐.

7. Circle the words that are missing. ***must have*** ***should not*** ***are not***

   We _____ left the door unlocked!

8. Circle the word that rhymes with ***noise***.

   toast toys night

9. Circle the correct word. ***plain*** ***plane***

   The biscuits were very _____.

10. Add punctuation.

    dave wasnt allowed to come to the skate park

11. Circle the nouns.

    Take the pen and some paper.

12. Write the missing verb. ***wrote*** ***painted***

    I ☐ *a picture at school today.*

MY SCORE

Day 5

1. ***I*** or ***me***?

   Dad and ☐ *like to play cricket.*

2. Circle the missing word. ***he*** ***him***

   Jack asked if I wanted to come with _____.

3. Write the jumbled word correctly.

   Make sure the rspea tyre is in the car. ☐

4. Which one is not a word?

   rebuild reapply rewent

5. Add ***less*** or ***ness*** to make a new word.

   sticky☐

6. Shorten ***has not***. ☐

7. Add the negative form of ***was*** to the sentence.

   Mum ☐ *happy with my school report.*

8. Circle the rhyming word. ***their***

   where cart then

9. Circle the correct word. ***whether*** ***weather***

   The _____ is lovely today.

10. Circle the missing word. ***Where's*** ***Wheres***

    _____ the best place to pitch the tent?

11. Circle the nouns.

    Athletes are very fit people.

12. Circle the verb.

    Francis spoke quickly.

WEEK 15

Skill focus

Commas for lists

A **comma** is a type of punctuation mark used in sentences to show a short pause.

This helps make the meaning of a sentence clearer.

A comma looks like this:

Commas are often used to separate items in a list.

A comma is used between every word or group of words in the list except the last two.

The word **and** or **or** goes between the last two items.

For example:

*We need hammers, nails, glue **and** a saw.*

Practice questions

1. Put in a comma (,).

   Mum cooked bacon eggs and tomato for dinner.

2. Put a dot where the word ***or*** should go.

   Would you like chocolate, vanilla strawberry cake for your birthday?

Day 1

1. Put in a comma (,).

   We need to buy bread milk and butter.

2. Put a dot where ***and*** should go.

   For Christmas, I asked for a bike, book football.

3. Add the word with the correct spelling. ***braken*** ***broken***

   The doctor said my arm was ______.

4. Number in alphabetical order.

   century ☐ certain ☐ centre ☐

5. Circle the words that are shortened to make ***don't***.

   do not done not do have

6. Circle the plural form of ***fish***.

   fishs fish

7. Circle the opposite words.

   tame pet wild

8. ***who's*** or ***whose***?

   Check ______ *at the door.*

9. Add punctuation.

   emma isnt a very friendly person

10. Cross out the word that is not needed.

    Jackie likes to eat soup when she thinks is feeling unwell.

11. Circle the missing word. ***you*** ***we***

    Do ______ know what the time is?

12. Circle a present tense form of ***visited***.

    visitde visitor visit

Day 2

1. Put in a comma (,).

   I packed water fruit and a map before our walk.

2. Put a dot where ***or*** should go.

   Would you like to go to the cinema, shop, pool museum?

3. Add the word with the correct spelling. ***hairy*** ***harey***

   The big, [ ] spider crawled across the table.

4. Circle the words that are shortened to make ***who's***.

   who is   who had

5. Circle the missing word. ***can*** ***can't***

   I _____ believe how tall you are!

6. Write the singular form of ***puppies***.

   [ ]

7. Circle the word closest in meaning to ***sparkling***.

   inventing   twinkling   disturbing

8. ***who's*** or ***whose***?

   The man [ ] finger is missing.

9. Add punctuation.

   who hasnt returned their homework

10. Circle which word doesn't belong.

    Gemma is always sleeping tired because she goes to bed too late.

11. Circle which word can replace the underlined ones. ***he*** ***him*** ***it*** ***that***

    Raj's hat is bright red; Raj got <u>the hat</u> yesterday.

12. Circle the missing verb. ***feel*** ***feels***

    We need to leave because John _____ sick.

MY SCORE

Day 3

1. Add punctuation to the sentence.

   We eat popcorn chocolate and ice cream at the cinema.

2. Put a dot where ***and*** should go.

   My best friends are Maggie, Jack Kate.

3. Rewrite the misspelt word correctly.

   There are seven difrent colours in a rainbow. [ ]

4. Number the words in alphabetical order.

   perhaps [ ]   peculiar [ ]

   particular [ ]

5. ***Aren't*** means [ ].

6. Write the plural form of ***elf***. [ ]

7. The opposite of ***give*** is [ ].

8. ***Who's*** or ***Whose***?

   [ ] *on the phone?*

9. Add punctuation.

   Stop! you didnt ask to use that

10. Cross out the word that is not needed.

    Can I please look at you your photographs?

11. Circle the missing word. ***it*** ***they***

    My cat had five kittens; _____ sleep a lot.

12. Circle a past tense form of ***wish***.

    wisht   wished   wishest

WEEK 15

Day 4

1. Add punctuation to the sentence.

   On Friday, we will visit Tom Mary Sam and Jane

2. Put a dot where ***or*** should go.

   The children could choose from nuggets, a burger pasta.

3. Circle and rewrite the misspelt word.

   My older brother turns therteen on Friday.

4. Circle the words that make ***who's***.

   who has who have

5. Circle the missing word. ***can can't***

   I ____ reach because I'm too short.

6. Write the singular form of ***leaves***.

7. Circle the word closest in meaning to ***intelligent***.

   bewildered exhausted clever

8. ***who's*** or ***whose***?

   Ask the man ______ wearing the blue jacket.

9. Add punctuation.

   my dog patches wont play ball with me

10. Cross out the word that is not needed.

    My dogs bark when someone comes beside to the door.

11. Circle which word can replace the underlined words. ***he him***

    My dad works in the library; my dad loves to read.

12. Circle the missing verb.

    eats eaten

    Natalie has ____ already.

MY SCORE

Day 5

1. Add punctuation.

   Please bring paper pencils an eraser and a pen.

2. Put a dot where ***and*** should go.

   I packed my hat, sunscreen, towel swimsuit for our trip to the beach.

3. Circle and rewrite the jumbled word.

   My parents own a small naravac.

4. Write in alphabetical order.

   strange strength straight

5. Shorten ***were not***.

6. Circle the plural form of ***story***.

   stories storys

7. The opposite of ***far*** is ______.

8. ***who's*** or ***whose***?

   Where's the cat ______ just had kittens?

9. Add punctuation.

   do you think ill get a new bike for christmas

10. Cross out the word that is not needed.

    I know my 10 times tables and chairs so does Joe.

11. Circle the correct word. ***it them***

    Lisa likes ____ when James tells funny jokes.

12. Circle a present tense form of ***felt***.

    am feeling was feeling

MY SCORE

WEEK 16

Day 1

1. Add the word with the correct spelling. ***biznes*** ***business***

   My parents have their own ______.

2. Make this word mean the opposite. ***re*** ***un***

   ______aware

3. ***laugh*** + ***ed*** = ______

4. Circle the plural of ***country***.

   countries countrys

5. Circle the missing word. ***can*** ***can't***

   I ____ swim very well; I need more lessons.

6. The opposite of ***push*** is ______.

7. ***was*** or ***were***?

   Dad ______ *in the army when he was younger.*

8. ***it's*** or ***its***?

   When ______ *cold, I wear my gloves.*

9. Punctuate.

   take out the flour sugar butter and milk

10. Rewrite the two proper nouns with capital letters.

    paris and new york are big cities.

11. Circle the correct word. ***it*** ***them***

    The tree had no leaves on ____ in autumn.

12. Statement ◯ or question ◯?

    Have you unpacked your school bag?

MY SCORE

Day 2

1. Add the word with the correct spelling. ***oposit*** ***opposite***

   The ______ *of yes is no.*

2. Add three letters.

   The ______*marine descended to the bottom of the ocean.*

3. What is the correct spelling for ***save*** + ***ing***? ______

4. Circle the plural form of ***man***.

   man mans men

5. Circle the missing word. ***can't*** ***haven't***

   Joey ____ watch that show; he's too young.

6. The opposite of ***long*** is ______.

7. ***is*** or ***are***?

   Amy's shoes ______ *pink and purple.*

8. ***your*** or ***you're***?

   Write ______ *name.*

9. Punctuate.

   My favourite colours are red blue and green.

10. Rewrite the two proper nouns with capital letters.

    The nile is a river in africa.

11. Put one word into the blank space.

    Jim and Fred are friends; ____ play football together.

12. Command ◯ or question ◯?

    Go to your room!

WEEK 16

Day 3

1. Add the word with the correct spelling. ***laff*** ***laugh***

   My brother has a loud ☐.

2. Make a new word. ***sub*** ***un***

   ☐load

3. ***final*** + ***ly*** = ☐

4. Circle the plural form of ***person***.

   persones people

5. Circle the missing word. ***wasn't*** ***can't***

   Ivan ____ at the game on Sunday.

6. Circle the opposite of ***alive***.

   healthy dead sick

7. ***was*** or ***were***?

   I thought you ☐ *Philip.*

8. ***Its*** or ***It's***?

   Are you coming to my party? ☐ *this Saturday.*

9. Punctuate.

   Tim Mandy Gina and James are going to the cinema.

10. Rewrite the two proper nouns that need capital letters.

    sydney is on the parramatta river.

    ☐ ☐

11. Circle the missing word. ***it*** ***them***

    My lunchbox has a cartoon character on ____.

12. Statement ☐ or question ☐?

    My mum is a very good cook.

MY SCORE

Day 4

1. Add the word with the correct spelling. ***bruz*** ***bruise***

   I have a large ☐ *on my knee.*

2. Add two letters.

   I had to ☐*write my name so I could read it.*

3. What is the correct spelling for ***write*** + ***ing***? ☐

4. Circle the plural form of ***deer***.

   deers deer

5. Write the missing word. ***can*** ***can't***

   I ☐ *fly, though I wish I could!*

6. Circle the opposite of ***stale***.

   might fresh young

7. ***is*** or ***are***?

   Where ☐ *you going?*

8. ***Your*** or ***You're***?

   ☐ *very tall!*

9. Punctuate.

   I have visited italy france and spain.

10. Rewrite the two words that need capital letters.

    tokyo is the capital city of japan.

    ☐ ☐

11. Put one word into the blank space.

    Sarah is learning to swim; ☐ *goes to lessons every week.*

12. Command ☐ or question ☐?

    Do you like eating pizza?

MY SCORE

Day 5

1. Add the word with the correct spelling. ***teche*** ***teach***

   I will [ ] *my little sister how to ride a bike.*

2. Make this word mean the opposite. ***re*** ***un***

   [ ]friendly

3. ***messy*** + ***ly*** = [ ]

4. Circle the singular form of ***adults***.

   adult people

5. Circle the missing word. ***can't*** ***haven't***

   I ____ been to your house before.

6. Circle the opposite of ***fiction***.

   story fact

7. ***was*** or ***were***?

   I thought you [ ] *Philip.*

8. ***its*** or ***it's***?

   My pet crab escaped from [ ] *tank.*

9. Punctuate.

   dad made a roast with potatoes carrots peas and gravy.

10. Circle the missing word. ***he*** ***him***

    I need to buy ____ a birthday present.

11. Circle the correct word. ***it*** ***they***

    The dog ran and ran until ____ was very tired.

12. Statement [ ] or command [ ]?

    Mix the milk with the flour.

Skill focus review

WEEK 16

1. Circle and rewrite the misspelt word.

   The house has a sqware door. [ ]

2. Circle two words close in meaning to ***difficult***.

   hard challenging easy

3. Circle the correct spelling of ***sew*** + ***ing***.

   sewwing sewing

4. Write the plural form of ***tooth***.

   [ ]

5. Add ***sub*** or ***re*** to make a new word.

   [ ]wind

6. Which words make the shortened word ***won't***?

   won not we will will not

7. The scissors belong to [ ].

   Did you return Ava's scissors after you used them?

8. Add a comma.

   I like reading books about dragons unicorns and fairies.

9. Circle the verb group.

   My aunt is having a baby next month.

10. Add the negative form of ***could***.

    I tried but I [ ] *reach the top shelf.*

11. ***he*** or ***him***?

    I went to the park with [ ].

12. Circle the word that can replace the underlined ones. ***they*** ***it***

    The birds sing in the morning; <u>the birds</u> are noisy.

Skill focus

Tricky verbs

A **verb** is a word that shows an action or tells about being or having.

Verbs can have different **tenses**. This tells us:

- if something has happened in the **past**;
- if something is happening in the **present**; or
- if something will happen in the **future**.

Usually, an ending like ***ed*** or ***ing*** is added to verbs when they change tense. The base word stays the same.

However, some verbs have different forms depending on whether they are past, present or future.

past	present	future
caught	catch	will catch
bought	buy	will buy
spoke	speak	will speak

Can you think of any others?

Practice questions

1. Circle a past tense form of ***fight***.

   fighted   foughted   fought

2. Add the correct form of ***drive*** to the sentence.

   My older brother ______ *me to school.*

Day 1

1. Circle a past tense form of speak.

   speaked   spoke   spoked

2. Add the correct form of ***sleep*** to the sentence.

   My cat, Misty, ______ *for 16 hours a day!*

3. Circle and rewrite the misspelt word.

   When will you retern those DVDs? ______

4. Write in alphabetical order.

   fibre   film   first

   ______ ______ ______

5. ***inform*** + ***ation*** = ______

6. Circle the plural form of ***piece***.

   peices   pieces   pieceys

7. Circle the opposite of ***whole***.

   all   part   every

8. ***your*** or ***you're***?

   Take out ______ *workbooks.*

9. Circle the phrase that is not correct.

   five dogs   Bobs lunch   tall trees

10. Circle the correct word. ***they*** ***we***

    Mum and Dad like music; ______ *often go to concerts.*

11. Circle the missing noun.
    berry   ***berries***

    Fiona and Max like collecting ______.

12. ***I*** or ***me***?

    This book was given to ______ *but* ______ *don't want it.*

Day 2

1. Circle a present tense form of ***blew***.

   blowed   blowen   blows

2. Circle the tense this sentence is written in. ***past*** ***present*** ***future***

   Heather ate her lunch in a hurry.

3. Circle and rewrite the misspelt word.

   We hear the chirch bells every Sunday. [ ]

4. Add the negative form of ***can***.

   My dog [ ] *walk because its leg is broken.*

5. Make this word mean the opposite.
   re ***un***

   [ ]fair

6. Circle the singular form of ***whales***.

   wale   whale

7. ***his*** or ***he's***?

   I liked [ ] *story, it was funny.*

8. ***its*** or ***it's***?

   The dog chewed [ ] *bone.*

9. Add punctuation.

   Jim Kate Sam and I are friends.

10. Write the missing words. ***we*** or ***us***.

    When we leave, you can come with [ ].

11. Circle the missing noun.
    sheep ***cattle***

    My cousin lives on a farm; she has a pet ____.

12. Write the missing words. ***them*** ***us***

    We took [ ] *to the zoo with* [ ].

MY SCORE

Day 3

1. What is the past tense form of ***hear***?

   heared   heart   heard

2. Add the correct form of ***bring***.

   I [ ] *my new toy to school.*

3. Circle and rewrite the misspelt word.

   We watched the meat sizle on the barbecue. [ ]

4. Write in alphabetical order.

   photo   phone   phonics

   [ ] [ ] [ ]

5. What is the correct spelling for ***imagine*** + ***ation***? [ ]

6. Circle the plural of ***bicycle***.

   bicycls   bicycles

7. Which word means ***to take*** or ***receive***?

   accept   except

8. ***there***, ***their*** or ***they're***?

   I'll call you when I get [ ].

9. The wing belongs to [ ].

   The bird's wing was injured.

10. Circle the missing word.
    they ***their*** ***them***

    I go to school with ____.

11. Circle the missing noun.
    computer ***rollerblades***

    Abdul got a new ____ for his birthday.

12. ***I*** or ***me***?

    Jo and [ ] *are good friends; she helps* [ ] *with my homework.*

MY SCORE

WEEK 17

WEEK 17

Day 4

1. Circle a present tense form of ***wrote***.
writed written writes

2. Circle the tense this sentence is written in. ***past present future***
My sister took me to the cinema.

3. Add the word with the correct spelling. ***fisical physical***
My favourite subject is ______ *fitness.*

4. Add the negative form of ***were***.
Jan and Steven ______ *far from home.*

5. Make this word mean the opposite.
re un
______kind

6. Circle the plural of ***monkey***.
monkies monkeys

7. ***his*** or ***he's***?
Do you know if ______ *coming?*

8. ***its*** or ***it's***?
I wear gloves when ______ *cold.*

9. Punctuate.
you will need your book scissors and glue

10. Write the missing words. ***he him***
I saw ______ *when* ______ *was riding past.*

11. Circle the missing noun. ***books book***
Ella puts the ______ *on the shelves.*

12. Write the missing words. ***them us***
We asked ______ *nicely, but they didn't help* ______.

MY SCORE

Day 5

1. Circle the past tense form of ***bring***.
brought bringed brung

2. Add the correct form of ***fly***.
The plane ______ *over the mountains.*

3. Circle and rewrite the misspelt word.
It was a plezure meeting you. ______

4. Number in alphabetical order.
price ☐ princess ☐ pretty ☐

5. Add ***ation*** to one word to make a noun.
limit crash believe
______

6. Circle the plural form of ***journey***.
journeyes journeys journies

7. Circle the opposite of ***everything***.
never nothing nowhere

8. ***your*** or ***you're***?
Please take ______ *bag.*

9. Circle the phrase that is not correct.
Conors mum box of oranges
red balls

10. Circle the correct word. ***they them***
Dara spoke to ______ *yesterday.*

11. Circle the missing noun.
pea broccoli
Chris really doesn't like ______.

12. ***I*** or ***me***?
Dad likes to sing with ______ *on stage but* ______ *am very shy.*

MY SCORE

Skill focus

Speech marks

When we write the words that someone has actually said, we put little marks around those words.

These marks are called **speech marks**.

Speech marks look like this:

Speech marks are like hands that hold the words being spoken.

They show where the speaker's words begin and end.

Any question marks or exclamation marks that are part of the speaker's words must also be included in the speech marks.

Practice questions

1. Add speech marks.

   Has anybody seen the cat? asked Mum.

2. Who is speaking? [ ]

   Emma replied, 'I think she's under the bed'.

Day 1

WEEK 18

1. Add speech marks.

   Mr Murphy asked, Where is your English book?

2. Who is speaking? [ ]

   'I think I left it at home', said Johnny.

3. Add the word with the correct spelling. ***wealty*** ***wealthy***

   My [ ] aunt lives in a mansion.

4. Which word can be added to ***body***?

   one every

5. ***sense*** + ***ation*** = [ ]

6. What is the base word of ***slept*** and ***sleeping***?

   [ ]

7. Which word is NOT the opposite of ***plain***?

   colourful ordinary fancy

8. ***to***, ***too*** or ***two***?

   You will need [ ] pens.

9. Add capital letters.

   jenny robbins is my neighbour.

10. Circle the mistake.

    We looked at Ben's holidays photographs.

11. Circle the adjectives that describe the noun.

    The short, chubby clown smiled at us.

12. ***I*** or ***me***?

    Jim and [ ] went to the park.

Day 2

1. Add speech marks.
   Can I get a new football? Tom asked.
2. Who is speaking? [ ]
   Tom's mum answered crossly, 'You already have three at home!'
3. Write the jumbled word correctly.
   I was a special tsuge at the ceremony. [ ]
4. Circle the rhyming words.
   square there ajar
5. Make this word mean **do again**.
   re ***un*** [ ] play
6. What is the base word of ***seen*** and ***seeing***? [ ]
7. ***have*** or ***of***? *Hint: have is used after should, would or could.*
   I took care [ ] *our class pet this week.*
8. ***by***, ***bye*** or ***buy***?
   Did you see the bus go [ ]*?*
9. Punctuate (' . ? !).
   Why doesnt Jim like dogs
10. Rewrite in the correct order.
    out. I'm going [ ]
11. Circle the correct word. ***every*** ***only***
    We like going on family picnics _____ month.
12. Which word can replace the underlined words? ***they*** ***we***
    Alison and I go to karate together and Alison and I are getting better.

MY SCORE

Day 3

1. Add speech marks.
   Watch out! the man shouted.
2. Who is speaking? [ ]
   'Thanks for the warning!' replied Anna gratefully.
3. Circle and rewrite the misspelt word.
   The little boy stuck his tunge out at the girl. [ ]
4. Circle the word you can add to ***ball***.
   round volley
5. ***prepare*** + ***ation*** = [ ]
6. What is the base word of ***sang*** and ***singing***? [ ]
7. Circle the opposites.
   question ask answer
8. ***to***, ***too*** or ***two***?
   I ate [ ] *apples today.*
9. Add punctuation.
   we fed the dogs and the birds before we left
10. Circle the mistake.
    Jake often read comics.
11. Circle the better word.
    obedient ***naughty***
    The _____ puppies ran away.
12. ***I*** or ***me***?
    Are you coming with [ ]*?*

MY SCORE

Day 4

1. Add speech marks.

   Good evening! the lady on the TV announced.

2. Who is speaking? [ ]

   'Change the channel, this is boring!' complained Jill.

3. Circle and rewrite the misspelt word.

   Gess what I have in my hand! [ ]

4. Circle the rhyming words.

   though show now

5. Make this word mean ***fill again***.

   re ***un*** [ ]fill

6. What is the base word of ***met*** and ***meeting***? [ ]

7. ***have*** or ***of***?

   I would [ ] *been on time, but I missed the bus!*

8. ***by***, ***bye*** or ***buy***?

   What did you [ ] *for lunch?*

9. Punctuate.

   jennifers leaving tomorrow

10. Rewrite in the correct order.

    carefully John his bike. rides

    [ ]

11. Circle the word needed in the sentence. ***before*** ***after*** ***while***

    I watch TV ______ *I am eating.*

12. Which word can replace the underlined words? ***we*** ***us***

    That boy was unkind to Eddy and me. He pushed Eddy and me into the mud.

MY SCORE

Day 5

1. Add speech marks.

   Jim asked, Where is my pencil case?

2. Who is speaking? [ ]

   A helpful boy named Jack replied, 'You left it in the library'.

3. Write the jumbled word correctly.

   Orange is my favourite locuro and I also like green. [ ]

4. Which word can be added to make a new word? ***time*** ***chair***

   [ ]table

5. ***admire*** + ***ation*** = [ ]

6. What is the base word of ***caught*** and ***catching***? [ ]

7. Which word is NOT the opposite of ***messy***?

   dirty tidy clean

8. ***meat*** or ***meet***?

   Cook the [ ] *in the oven.*

9. Rewrite the two words that need capital letters.

   athens is the capital city of greece.

   [ ] [ ]

10. Circle the mistake.

    Quick! Bring a ladder, the cat's stucks in that tree!

11. Circle the adjectives.

    Mum's car is red and shiny.

12. ***I*** or ***me***?

    Mum and [ ] *like playing tennis.*

MY SCORE

Skill focus

Why do we add *mis-* and *dis-* to words?

Sometimes, groups of letters are added to the beginning of words.

This makes a new word which has a different meaning from the **base word**.

A **base word** is a word that doesn't have any word parts added to it.

The word part ***mis*** means ***bad*** or ***wrong***.

behave ⟶ misbehave spell ⟶ misspell

The word part ***dis*** means ***not***. They make the base word its opposite.

approve ⟶ disapprove appear ⟶ disappear

Not all word parts can be added to the beginning of every word.

To help you decide whether to use ***mis*** or ***dis***, try adding them both to the base word.

Then, read each word aloud to decide which one sounds right.

Practice questions

1. Add ***mis*** or ***dis***.

spell

2. Is the word used correctly?

yes ◯ no ◯

I am good at spelling. I misspell many words.

Day 1

1. Add ***mis*** or ***dis***. ☐respect
2. Is the underlined word used correctly? yes ◯ no ◯
   The man was very polite to the woman. He disrespected her.
3. Write the jumbled word correctly.
   Light the ndleca carefully, we need some light! ☐
4. Circle the letters left out of these shortened words. ***he'll it'll they'll***
   ca no wi
5. ***poison*** + ***ous*** = ☐
6. Change the ending to make this word mean the ***most angry***.
   angrier ☐
7. The opposite of ***lost*** is ☐.
8. ***shore*** or ***sure***?
   Are you ☐ *it's cooked?*
9. Add speech marks.
   Where are you going? questioned my mum.
10. Who is speaking? ☐
    'Can we go to the pool now, Mum?' Ben asked.
11. Circle the missing verb. ***typed type***
    My grandpa said I can _____ really fast.
12. Circle the proper noun.
    Venus was visible.

WEEK 19

Day 2

1. Add **mis** or **dis**. [ ]treat
2. Is the underlined word used correctly? yes [ ] no [ ]
   The lady looked after her dog well. She mistreats it.
3. Add the word with the correct spelling. ***centermeter*** ***centimetre***
   One [ ] *is very small.*
4. Which word can be added to make a new word? ***fish*** ***star***
   gold[ ]
5. Add **ous** to make a new word.
   faster danger [ ]
6. Circle the plural form of ***ice***.
   ice ices icies
7. ***have*** or ***of***?
   I should [ ] *baked a cake.*
8. ***hour*** or ***our***?
   Where did we park [ ] *car?*
9. Add speech marks.
   The shy girl asked, Would you like to play with me?
10. Punctuate.
   the highest mountain in ireland is in kerry
11. Circle the verb and rewrite in the present tense.
   I waited for the train. [ ]
12. Add the words in the correct places. ***sand*** ***art***
   pieces of [ ]
   grains of [ ]

MY SCORE

Day 3

1. Add **mis** or **dis**.
   [ ]agree
2. Is the underlined word used correctly? yes [ ] no [ ]
   You are right. I disagree with you.
3. Rewrite the misspelt word correctly.
   Jim will probly catch the bus with me. [ ]
4. Shorten ***had not***. [ ]
5. What is the correct spelling for ***fame*** + ***ous***? [ ]
6. Change the ending to make this word mean the ***most late***.
   later [ ]
7. The opposite of ***cry*** is [ ].
8. ***shore*** or ***sure***?
   Walk along the [ ].
9. Add speech marks.
   Mr Jones asked, Who knows the answer to this question?
10. Who is speaking? [ ]
   'Do you know where Mr Jones is?' Rosie asked Miss Brown.
11. Circle the missing verb. ***bring*** ***brought***
   Did you [ ] *your computer with you?*
12. Circle two nouns.
   Tea and coffee are available.

MY SCORE

Day 4

1. Add **mis** or **dis**. ______ *read*
2. Is the underlined word used correctly? yes ☐ no ☐
   I answered the question incorrectly. I misread it.
3. Circle and rewrite the misspelt word.
   The ship sailed into the harbour yesturday. ______
4. Circle the word you can add to **coat**.
   blue rain
5. **adventure** + **ous** = ______
6. Circle the plural form of **sheep**.
   sheeps sheepes sheep
7. **have** or **of**?
   We picked bunches ______ *flowers.*
8. **our** or **hour**?
   When will ______ *taxi be here?*
9. Add speech marks.
   I'm afraid of spiders! Billy cried.
10. Punctuate.
    the city of paris is in france.
11. Circle the verb and rewrite in the past tense.
    We walk to school. ______
12. Add the words in the correct places. **soap** **paper**
    a piece of ______
    a bar of ______

MY SCORE

Day 5

1. Add **mis** or **dis**. ______ *like*
2. Is the underlined word used correctly? yes ☐ no ☐
   That girl is not my friend. I dislike her.
3. Circle and rewrite the jumbled word.
   Mum called out, 'Be fuelrac' as I was crossing the road. ______
4. Shorten **must have**. ______
5. **vary** + **ous** = ______
   Hint: remember the rule for words ending with ***y***.
6. Change the ending to make this word mean the **most great**.
   greater ______
7. The opposite of **always** is ______.
8. Add **blew** and **blue** in the correct places.
   The boy ______ *a bubble and his gum was* ______*!*
9. Add speech marks.
   Who's coming with me? Dad asked.
10. Who is speaking? ______
    'Flynn and Rose are on the playground', Thomas told John.
11. Circle the missing verb. **drink drinks**
    My cat ____ *milk with her tongue.*
12. Circle the proper noun.
    Amy spreads the icing out evenly.

MY SCORE

Skill focus

Comparing good and bad

Adjectives are words that can be used to describe a noun:

*The **fast** car.*

*That **car** is **fast**.*

Adjectives can also be used to compare two or more things.

When we do this, we usually add er or est to the end of the word.

*This car is **fast**.*

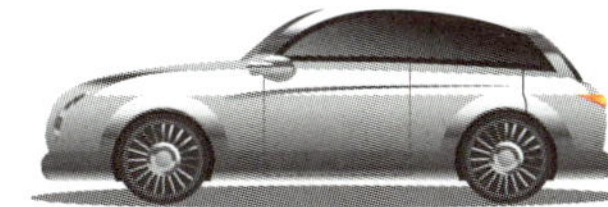

*This car is **faster**.*

*This car is **fastest**.*

However, some adjectives do not follow this rule. For example:

When we want to compare two **good** things, we use ***good***, ***better*** and ***best***.

When we want to compare two **bad** things, we use ***bad***, ***worse*** and ***worst***.

Practice questions

1. Write the adjective in the correct form. ***bad***

   My brother has the ______ *habits.*

2. Which word should replace the underlined words? ***worse*** ***worst***

   My first drawing was more bad than this one.

Day 1

1. Write the adjective in the correct form. ***good***

   The chefs judged Sam's cake as the ______ *of them all.*

2. Which word should replace the underlined words? ***better*** ***best***

   Sam has the most good cake.

3. Add the word with the correct spelling. ***evening*** ***evning***

   We play basketball at the park every ______.

4. Circle the rhyming words.

   hurry carry worry

5. Make this word mean 'to not behave'. ***mis*** ***dis***

   ______behave

6. ***admire*** + ***ation*** = ______

7. Circle the singular form of ***libraries***.

   librarie libry library

8. ***was*** or ***were***?

   When ______ *your birthday?*

9. Circle the missing word. ***great*** ***grate***

   Please ____ *the carrot for the salad.*

10. Add speech marks.

    Did you look outside? said Mum.

11. Cross out the word that doesn't belong.

    The cup and the plate and were on the table.

12. Circle the tense this sentence is written in. ***past*** ***present*** ***future***

    Jeremy is running and Kevin is walking.

WEEK 20

Day 2

1. Write ***bad*** in the correct form.

   This weather is the ______ *!*

2. Which word should replace the underlined words? ***worse*** ***worst***

   I have had the most bad day today.

3. Circle and rewrite the misspelt word.

   The children were cleening the car. ______

4. Write in alphabetical order.

   wake waste wait

   ______ ______ ______

5. Add ***ation*** to one word.

   watch prepare ______

6. Which one is not a word?

   graduation fasteration

7. Circle the plural of ***language***.

   languagies languages

8. Circle a word with a similar meaning to ***brave***.

   discover heroic instantly

9. Add ***sail*** and ***sale*** in the correct places.

   I bought a cheap ______ *for my boat in a boat* ______.

10. Add speech marks.

    What is your name? asked the boy.

11. Rewrite in the correct order. Punctuate.

    the tree from apple the fell

    ______

12. Circle a past tense form of ***catch***.

    catches catched caught

MY SCORE

Day 3

1. Write the adjective in the correct form. ***good***

   My drawing was ______ *than last time.*

2. Which word should replace the underlined words? ***better*** ***best***

   Pencils are more good for drawing than crayons.

3. Circle and rewrite the misspelt word.

   Ali was yousing the broom to sweep the floor. ______

4. Circle the rhyming words.

   strength width length

5. Make this word mean 'not in order'. ***dis*** ***un***

   ______order

6. ***care*** + ***less*** + ***ly*** = ______

7. One shelf, two ______.

8. ***seen*** or ***saw***?

   I thought I ______ *a shooting star.*

9. Add the word ***seen*** or ***scene***.

   Have you ______ *that film?*

10. Add speech marks.

    Do you have the time, please? the stranger asked.

11. Which word doesn't belong? Circle it.

    Jane and I was were going to play tennis.

12. Circle the tense this sentence is written in. ***past*** ***present*** ***future***

    My grandmother was born in Russia.

MY SCORE

WEEK 20

Day 4

1. Write ***bad*** in the correct form.

   My sandwich is [ ] *than my sister's.*

2. Which word should replace the underlined words? ***worse*** ***worst***

   I feel more bad than yesterday.

3. Circle and rewrite the misspelt word.

   The yooth of today know how to use computers. [ ]

4. Write in alphabetical order.

   often over oven

   [ ] [ ] [ ]

5. Circle the correct spelling of ***use*** + ***able***. useabel usable

6. Make a new word. ***able*** ***en***

   respect[ ]

7. Circle the plural form of ***bridge***.

   bridgs bridges

8. Circle a word with a similar meaning to ***created***.

   challenged pretended invented

9. Circle the word that fits.

   meddle ***medal***

   An Olympic gold [ ].

10. Add speech marks.

    Look at that rainbow! the children said excitedly.

11. Rewrite in the correct order. Punctuate.

    i fly helicopter saw by a

    [ ]

12. Circle a present tense form of ***cooked***.

    is cooking was cooking

MY SCORE

Day 5

1. Write ***good*** in the correct form.

   I am the [ ] *player in my football team.*

2. Which word should replace the underlined words? ***better*** ***best***

   This is my most good friend.

3. Circle and rewrite the misspelt word.

   Bewty and the beast is a popular fairytale. [ ]

4. Circle the word that rhymes with ***calf***.

   laugh stuff cast

5. Make this word mean the opposite.

   mis ***un***

   [ ]spell

6. ***invent*** + ***ion*** = [ ]

7. One party, two [ ].

8. ***was*** or ***were***?

   Kate and Jen [ ] *laughing.*

9. Add the words. ***plane*** ***plain***

   The seats on the [ ]

   were very [ ].

10. Add speech marks.

    I asked Mum, What's for lunch?

11. Cross out the word that doesn't belong.

    The motorbikes roared past us then noisily.

12. Circle the tense this sentence is written in. ***past*** ***present*** ***future***

    I really enjoyed my meal at lunchtime.

MY SCORE

WEEK 21

Skill focus

Words that tell us how and when

Some words can be used to tell how and when things happen. These are known as **adverbs**.

They are used to change or add more information to the verb.

These words help make our writing clearer and more interesting.

<u>**After**</u> we eat, we will <u>**quickly**</u> wash the dishes.
when how

There are many other words that can be used to tell when a verb happens:

The words that tell us how the verb happens usually end with ***ly***:

Practice questions

1. Circle the word needed to finish the sentence. ***constantly eventually***
   She is quite slow, but she will _____ finish her dinner.
2. Write the word that tells how they drove. [ ]
   They drove sadly to the airport.

Day 1

1. Circle the word needed to finish the sentence. ***Before After During***
   _____ dinner, I brush my teeth then go to bed.
2. Write the word that tells how Francis spoke. [ ]
   Francis spoke quickly.
3. Write the jumbled word correctly.
   There was dunerth and lightning during the stormy night.
   [ ]
4. Circle the word that rhymes with ***first***.
   coast burst rest
5. Add three letters to the word.
   Don't forget to [ ]connect the internet when you log off.
6. Change the ending to make this word mean the ***most ugly***.
   uglier [ ]
7. ***is*** or ***are***?
   My friend [ ] over there.
8. ***who's*** or ***whose***?
   Where's the cat [ ] just had kittens?
9. The jacket belongs to [ ].
   Bobby's new jacket looks warm.
10. Which word doesn't belong? Circle it.
    My instant birthday is in February.
11. Command [ ], question [ ] or statement [ ]?
    Blue is my favourite colour.
12. Circle the verb group.
    Gran is coming to dinner.

Day 2

1. Circle the word needed to finish the sentence. ***suddenly*** ***finally***

   The bus stopped ____ at the light.

2. Write the word that tells how the web page loaded. [ ]

   The web page loaded slowly.

3. Circle and rewrite the misspelt word.

   I like dogs, althow big dogs scare me. [ ]

4. Add the negative form of ***is***.

   Tim [ ] *feeling well.*

5. Circle the correct spelling of ***believe*** + ***able***.

   belivable believable

6. Write ***good*** in the correct form.

   Their performance today was [ ] *than last time.*

7. Circle the opposite of ***serious***.

   quiet smart silly

8. ***your*** or ***you're***?

   If [ ] *thirsty, have a drink.*

9. Punctuate.

   the children werent behaving very well on the school trip

10. Circle which word doesn't belong.

    I am cooked dinner for my family.

11. Circle the words that are missing. ***might have*** ***must have***

    Joey ____ been here before, though I'm not sure.

12. Circle the present tense form of ***He was going***.

    He will go He went He is going

MY SCORE

Day 3

1. Circle the word needed to finish the sentence. ***during*** ***while***

   The canteen is open ____ lunch.

2. Write the word that tells how Dad yelled. [ ]

   Dad yelled at us crossly.

3. Write the jumbled word correctly.

   The shoes and the jacket were made of tlaerhe. [ ]

4. Circle two rhyming words.

   shirt curse hurt

5. Add three letters to this word.

   If you [ ] *obey the rules you will be punished.*

6. Change the ending to make this word mean the ***most fresh***.

   fresher [ ]

7. Circle the missing word. ***has*** ***have*** ***having***

   I ____ to clean my room each week.

8. ***who's*** or ***whose***?

   Catch the kitten [ ] *tail is black.*

9. The tail belongs to [ ].

   The dog's tail wagged furiously.

10. Circle which word doesn't belong.

    Put the note not on the fridge.

11. Command [ ], question [ ] or statement [ ]?

    Move away from the road!

12. Circle the verb group.

    I will make a sandwich.

MY SCORE

WEEK 21

WEEK 21

Day 4

1. Circle the word needed to finish the sentence. ***suddenly*** ***finally***

   The ship ____ reached its destination, after many months at sea.

2. Write the word that tells how she burst into song. [ ]

   She burst into song joyfully.

3. Write the jumbled word correctly.

   The toy dersiol was lying on the floor. [ ]

4. Add the negative form of ***was***.

   The bird [ ] *in its cage this morning.*

5. Circle the correct spelling of ***permit*** + ***ion***. permition permission

6. Write the correct form of ***bad***.

   The hotel room was bad and the meal was [ ].

7. Circle the opposite of ***cooked***.

   toasted raw boiled

8. Add the words. ***your*** ***you're***

   Go and wash [ ] *hands,* [ ] *all dirty!*

9. Punctuate.

   declan didnt eat his lunch

10. Circle which word doesn't belong.

    She would lives in an old cottage.

11. Circle the words that are missing. ***mustn't have*** ***must have***

    Mum ____ fed the dogs because they seem hungry!

12. Circle the past tense form of ***She is singing***.

    She sings She was singing

MY SCORE

Day 5

1. Circle the word needed to finish the sentence. ***while*** ***after***

   We like to talk about our day ____ dinner.

2. Write the word that tells how the dogs ate. [ ]

   The dogs ate greedily.

3. Circle and rewrite the misspelt word.

   I like to watch magicians perform magik. [ ]

4. Circle the rhyming words.

   ghost past toast grown

5. Add three letters to the word.

   The magician made the rabbit [ ]*appear.*

6. Change the ending to make this word mean the ***most scary***.

   scarier [ ]

7. ***seen*** or ***saw***?

   I haven't [ ] *your jacket.*

8. ***Who's*** or ***Whose***?

   [ ] *invited to the party?*

9. Circle the missing word. ***Tara's*** ***Taras***

   Where is ____ hat?

10. Circle which word doesn't belong.

    Please put that book then on the bottom shelf.

11. This sentence is a: command [ ], question [ ] or a statement [ ]?

    Do you want sausages for dinner?

12. Circle the verb group.

    Jane was laughing at the funny joke.

MY SCORE

Skill focus

Conjunctions

When we want to show that two parts of a sentence are connected, we use a joining word. These words are known as **conjunctions**.

You may know the conjunctions ***and***, ***or*** and ***but***.

These words can be used in the middle of a sentence to join words or ideas:

*I went to the park, **and** I played on the swings.*

*The fruit looked fresh, **but** it was rotten.*

*Would you like to walk to school, **or** do you want to ride your bike?*

Usually, the two parts of the sentence that are joined by these words make sense on their own.

Another useful conjunction is ***because***. It is used to give a reason why something happens:

*Billy was sad **because** his brother wouldn't play with him.*

This type of conjunction connects one part of a sentence that makes sense on its own and another part that does not make sense on its own.

Practice questions

1. Circle the conjunction.

   We don't have any more eggs because Mum used them all in the cake.

2. Circle the word needed to finish the sentence. ***and*** or ***but***

   Our cousins visited us _____ they stayed over for the night.

Day 1

1. Circle the conjunction.

   I like swimming and playing football.

2. Circle the word needed to finish the sentence. ***and*** or ***but***

   I wanted to go swimming, _____ I forgot my swimsuit.

3. Circle and rewrite the jumbled word.

   The detective solved the ystrmye at the end of the story.

   [ ]

4. Circle the rhyming words.

   daughter water drought wait

5. ***save*** + ***ing*** = [ ]

6. Circle two words that can be built from ***make***.

   makest makey making made

7. Circle the singular form of ***people***.

   peoples peopl person

8. Circle the word with a similar meaning to ***recently***.

   tomorrow lately instantly

9. ***Its*** or ***It's***?

   [ ] *too hot today!*

10. Add two commas.

    Tomorrow, we will visit Kyle Norah Tim and Colin.

11. Add the correct form of ***listen***.

    Sarah [ ] *to music while she cleans.*

12. Tick the missing word.
    before ☐ ***finally*** ☐

    The plane _____ reached its destination.

Day 2

1. Circle the conjunction.

   We might go to the river or maybe to the lake.

2. Circle the word needed to finish the sentence. ***and*** or ***but***

   I have an older sister _____ a younger brother.

3. Add the word with the correct spelling. ***numbar*** ***number***

   Do you know your phone [ ]*?*

4. Write in alphabetical order.

   July junk June

   [ ] [ ] [ ]

5. Add ***ous*** to make a new word.

   mountain river [ ]

6. Circle two words that can be built from ***angry***.

   angrying angrily angries angrier

7. Write the plural form of ***pyramid***.

   [ ]

8. Circle the opposite of ***nothing***.

   everything everywhere everyone

9. ***your*** or ***you're***?

   I don't think [ ] *listening!*

10. Add speech marks.

    Where are you going? Ian called after them.

11. Circle the verb.

    Anna is a great nurse.

12. Write the word that tells ***how the child ran***. [ ]

    The child ran clumsily.

MY SCORE

Day 3

1. Circle the conjunction.

   Jonah likes kittens, but he doesn't like cats.

2. Circle the word needed to finish the sentence. ***and*** or ***but***

   You may do a painting _____ a drawing.

3. Add the word with the correct spelling. ***katalog*** ***catalogue***

   I love to look at the toy [ ]*.*

4. Circle the rhyming words.

   centre enter meet

5. Which one is not a word?

   meeted loved

6. Circle two words that can be built from ***seem***.

   seemingly seemest seems seemful

7. Write the singular form of ***skis***. [ ]

8. Circle the opposite of ***peaceful***.

   violent nice calm

9. ***there***, ***their*** or ***they're***?

   Look! Over [ ]*!*

10. Add two commas.

    Monkeys eat fruit leaves insects and flowers.

11. Add the correct form of ***dance***.

    I [ ] *for two hours at the party yesterday.*

12. Tick the missing word.

    suddenly [ ] ***finally*** [ ]

    We _____ went to bed after a very long day.

MY SCORE

Day 4

1. Circle the conjunction.

   Andrew went home because he felt homesick.

2. Circle the word needed to finish the sentence. ***and*** or ***but***

   We want to get a puppy, ______ there is no room in our house.

3. Add the word with the correct spelling. ***gathor*** ***gather***

   Please [ ] *all your belongings and follow me.*

4. Write in alphabetical order.

   probably practise

   [ ] [ ]

5. ***limit*** + ***ation*** = [ ]

6. Circle two words that can be built from ***love***.

   loving lovest loveliest loveful

7. Write the plural form of ***ocean***. [ ]

8. Circle two words similar in meaning to ***crying***.

   weeping sobbing frowning

9. ***your*** or ***you're***?

   Is Ben [ ] *cousin?*

10. Add speech marks.

    Brian, why isn't your room tidy yet? asked Dad.

11. Circle the verb.

    They went out for breakfast.

12. Write the word that tells how they finished their work. [ ]

    They finished their work easily.

Day 5

1. Circle the conjunction.

   We don't eat eggs because we are vegans.

2. Circle the word needed to finish the sentence. ***and*** or ***but***

   Suki can be rude sometimes, ______ she is a kind girl.

3. Add the word with the correct spelling. ***yott*** ***yacht***

   The [ ] *sailed by.*

4. Circle the rhyming words.

   sizzle drizzle scissors

5. Circle the correct spelling of ***face*** + ***ing***. faceing facing

6. Circle two words that can be built from ***care***.

   careful carey caring careness

7. Write the singular form of ***bottles***. [ ]

8. ***is*** or ***are***?

   The twins [ ] *turning nine tomorrow.*

9. ***its*** or ***it's***?

   The boat had no wind in [ ] *sails.*

10. Add two commas.

    This morning, we will be doing spelling writing reading and art.

11. Add the correct form of ***dream***.

    I was [ ] *about aliens.*

12. Tick the missing word.

    sometimes [ ] ***next*** [ ]

    Our grandpa ______ gives us pocket money.

WEEK 22

Skill focus

A or *an*?

The words ***a*** and ***an*** are used in sentences to tell us more about a noun:

*I wanted **a** cake for my birthday.*

*Mum asked me to bring her **an** egg.*

In these sentences, ***a*** and ***an*** tell us that we are talking about *any* cake or *any* egg.

Even though ***a*** and ***an*** are used in the same way, knowing when to use them can be tricky.

The word ***an*** is only used in front of a word that starts with a vowel sound.

We use ***a*** before words that start with a consonant. For example:

*I gave Mum **an** egg. I gave her **a** bag of flour too.*

Practice questions

1. ***a*** or ***an***?

   ☐ tree

2. Circle the word that correctly completes the sentence.
   amazing ***boring*** ***exciting***
   My mum bought us a _____ new video game.

Day 1

1. ***a*** or ***an***? ☐ ice cream
2. Circle the word that correctly completes the sentence.
   beach ***island*** ***city***
   We will visit an _____ on our holiday.
3. Add the word with the correct spelling. ***Januree*** ***January***
   My mum's birthday is in ☐.
4. Which word can be added to ***case***?
   boat book
5. Which one is not a word?
   going stopping ateing
6. Circle two words that can be built from ***shoot***.
   shootly shooting shot shooted
7. Which word is NOT similar in meaning to ***jump***?
   bound leap stand
8. ***meat*** or ***meet***?
   I am going to ☐ *the queen!*
9. Punctuate.
   Where do you think youre going the soldier demanded.
10. Circle the words that tell when they walked the dog.
    We walked the dog this morning.
11. Circle the conjunction.
    Mum bought me a new hat because my old one was torn.
12. Write the correct form of ***bad***.
    That was the ☐ *film I've ever seen.*

Day 2

1. ***a*** or ***an***? [ ] apple

2. Circle the word that correctly completes the sentence.
   apple ***vanilla*** ***enormous***
   I chose a ___ cake for my birthday.

3. Add the word with the correct spelling. ***lite*** ***light***
   I turned on the [ ] *so I could see better.*

4. ***It'll*** means [ ].

5. Add ***sub*** to make a new word.
   possible marine appear
   [ ]

6. Circle two words that can be built from ***happy***.
   happys happily happiest happied

7. Circle the missing word. ***am*** ***is*** ***are***
   Mary and Jody ___ twin sisters.

8. Which word? ***clause*** ***claws***
   The nails of a cat or tiger.

9. Circle the words that need a capital letter.
   geraldine thomas tomorrow

10. Write the word that tells how they completed their chores.
    [ ]
    We cheerfully completed our chores.

11. Circle the conjunction.
    I would like a pet dog, but my parents said no.

12. Circle the noun.
    The large jet took off.

MY SCORE

Day 3

1. ***a*** or ***an***? [ ] baby

2. Circle the word that correctly completes the sentence.
   cousin ***friend*** ***aunt***
   I have an ___ who lives in Hanoi.

3. Add the word with the correct spelling. ***breth*** ***breath***
   I took a deep [ ] *and tried again.*

4. Which word can be added to make a new word? ***light*** ***dark***
   [ ]house

5. Which one is not a word?
   useless useful useness

6. Circle two words that can be built from ***camp***.
   camped camply camping

7. Which word is NOT the opposite of ***finished***?
   started began ended

8. Add the word. ***which*** ***witch***
   The frightening [ ] *stirred her potion.*

9. Punctuate.
   Why didnt you come asked Mary.

10. Circle the words that tell when they went to bed.
    We went to bed late.

11. Circle the conjunction.
    Would you like lemonade or juice with your lunch?

12. Write the correct form of ***good***.
    We had the [ ] *holiday.*

MY SCORE

WEEK 23

WEEK 23

Day 4

1. ***a*** or ***an***? [ ] egg
2. Circle the word that correctly completes the sentence.
   orange ***pear*** ***peach***
   I ate an _____ and a banana after lunch.
3. Add the word with the correct spelling. ***ahed*** ***ahead***
   There was a dark cave [ ] *of us.*
4. Shorten ***will not***. [ ]
5. Add ***sub*** to make a new word.
   pay day way
   [ ]
6. Circle two words that can be built from ***taste***.
   tasteful tastely tasted tasteness
7. Circle the missing word. ***am is are***
   I _____ the youngest in my family.
8. Add the words ***aloud*** and ***allowed*** in the correct places.
   Reading [ ] *is not* [ ] *in the library.*
9. Which words need a capital letter?
   christmas wednesday month
10. Write the word that tells how they spoke. [ ]
    They spoke politely to the old man.
11. Circle the conjunction.
    My dad is very tall and his brother is too.
12. Circle the noun.
    They showed their fangs.

MY SCORE

Day 5

1. ***a*** or ***an***? [ ] present
2. Circle the word that correctly completes the sentence.
   gloves ***apron*** ***hat***
   I wear an _____ when I cook in the kitchen.
3. Add the word with the correct spelling. ***fule*** ***fuel***
   We put [ ] *in the car before we drove to the shop.*
4. Which word can be added to make a new word? ***spider*** ***site***
   web [ ]
5. Which one is not a word?
   joked speaked
6. Circle two words that can be built from ***need***.
   needy needment needs needly
7. Which word is NOT similar in meaning to ***draw***?
   scribble sketch glue
8. Add the word ***dye*** or ***die***.
   If you don't feed your fish they may [ ].
9. Punctuate.
   Theyre late complained Anna.
10. When do they visit India? Circle.
    Our family visits India yearly.
11. Circle the conjunction.
    Eat your green vegetables because they are good for you.
12. Add the correct form of ***early***.
    I ate an apple [ ].

MY SCORE

WEEK 24

Day 1

1. Add the word with the correct spelling. ***measure*** ***meshure***

   Can you help me ____ this piece of paper?

2. Circle the word that DOES NOT rhyme.

   liar higher tyre flower

3. ***dis*** + ***obey*** = ____

4. ***to***, ***too*** or ***two***?

   Will your sisters come  *?*

5. Circle two words similar in meaning.

   green emerald yellow

6. Add punctuation.

   the river seine flows through paris.

7. Add speech marks.

   Can I come too? the little girl asked.

8. Circle the mistake.

   Dad yelled cross at us.

9. ***I*** or ***me***?

   The dog followed ____ home.

10. ***a*** or ***an***?

11. Circle the conjunction.

    I went to the shop and bought the ingredients for dinner.

12. Circle one verb group and rewrite it in the present tense.

    The children were playing football.

    ____

Day 2

1. Add the word with the correct spelling. ***tho*** ***though***

   Even ____ it was raining, we still played outside.

2. Circle the rhyming words.

   tagged dragged rigged

3. ***humour*** + ***ous*** = ____

4. Add ***sale*** or ***sail***.

   Ron bought a model ____ boat in the toy ____.

5. ***go***, ***goes*** or ***gone***?

   Cara has ____ home.

6. Write the missing word. ***birds*** ***bird's***

   The ____ nest was destroyed by the strong winds.

7. Add speech marks.

   Are you the team's goalkeeper? she asked.

8. Circle which word doesn't belong.

   On Friday night, we are will watch a play.

9. ***we*** or ***us***?

   When are you coming to visit ____?

10. Which word correctly completes the sentence?

    amazing ***fantastic*** ***boring***

    The band put on an ____ show!

11. Circle the conjunction.

    Would you like to come with me or do you want to stay at home?

12. Circle a past tense form of ***writes***.

    have writed has written has wrote

WEEK 24

Day 3

1. Add the word with the correct spelling. ***ferst*** ***first***

   I came ☐ *in the running race.*

2. Circle the word that rhymes with ***dreaming***.

   flinging steaming cleaning

3. Make this word mean the opposite. ***dis*** ***un***

   ☐safe

4. Circle the word that means ***two of something***.

   pear pair

5. Circle the opposites.

   shy mean outgoing

6. Add punctuation.

   flora didnt bring any money to buy a ticket

7. Add speech marks.

   Will you be coming to my party? I asked my friends.

8. Circle the mistake.

   Check the computers is turned off.

9. ***I*** or ***me***?

   Can you tell ☐ *the secret?*

10. ***a*** or ***an***?

    ☐ endangered species

11. Circle the conjunction.

    I went to the park and I saw my friend there.

12. Circle one verb group and rewrite it in the present tense.

    I was cooking dinner.

    ☐

MY SCORE

Day 4

1. Add the word with the correct spelling. ***Febrooary*** ***February***

   Valentine's Day is in ☐.

2. Circle the word that rhymes with ***tracks***.

   index taxi tax

3. ***outrage*** + ***ous*** = ☐

4. ***so*** or ***sew***?

   I am learning to ☐ *at school.*

5. ***go***, ***goes*** or ***gone***?

   You can ☐ *first.*

6. Write the missing word. ***children*** ***children's***

   Where are the ☐ *parents?*

7. Add speech marks.

   Will the last remaining passengers please go to gate seven? the lady announced.

8. Circle which word doesn't belong.

   Kieran is in not from Ireland.

9. ***we*** or ***us***?

   When it's cold, ☐ *like to eat soup.*

10. Which word correctly completes the sentence?
    interesting ***slow*** ***boring***

    My new book was an ____ *read.*

11. Circle the conjunction.

    I like cats because they are cute.

12. Circle a past tense form of ***works***.

    was worked was working was work

MY SCORE

Day 5

1. Rewrite the misspelt word correctly.

   I knue you were joking! [ ]

2. Circle two rhyming words.

   tricks fix wax

3. Make this word mean the opposite. ***dis un***

   [ ]grateful

4. Write the correct word. ***wait weight***

   Lee couldn't [ ] to get on the scales and check his [ ].

5. Circle two words similar in meaning.

   frosty chilly humid

6. Add punctuation.

   the elephant was painting a picture with its trunk

7. Add speech marks.

   Let's go for a swim! she suggested.

8. Circle the mistake.

   The men cheers for their team.

9. ***I*** or ***me***?

   Mina came to visit my sister and [ ].

10. ***a*** or ***an***?

    [ ] terrible accident

11. Circle the conjunction.

    I like most vegetables, but I don't like cabbage.

12. Circle one verb group and rewrite it in the present tense.

    Fido was sleeping on the mat.

    [ ]

MY SCORE

Skill focus review

1. Circle and rewrite the misspelt word.

   They will probly be late because of the traffic. [ ]

2. Circle the two rhyming words.

   their stairs hair

3. Add ***mis*** or ***dis*** to make a new word.

   [ ]infect

4. Add ***ation*** to one word to make a noun.

   super begin inform

   [ ]

5. ***hour*** or ***our***?

   The lesson lasted for an [ ].

6. Circle the opposite of ***answer***.

   telling question asking

7. Add speech marks.

   Nelly warned the old lady, Watch out for that step!

8. Write the correct form of ***bad***.

   I am having the [ ] day ever!

9. Write the word that tells how the baby slept. [ ]

   The baby slept peacefully.

10. Which word correctly completes the sentence?

    sleepy angry energetic

    The _____ cat was lying on the bed.

11. Circle the conjunction.

    I will bring the ball and you can bring the bat.

12. Circle a past tense form of ***fly***.

    flew flied flewed

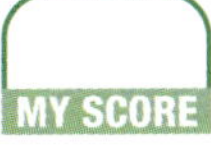

More conjunctions

When we want to show that two parts of a sentence are connected, we use a joining word. These are known as **conjunctions**.

Other than ***and***, ***or***, ***but*** and ***because***, there are many other conjunctions:

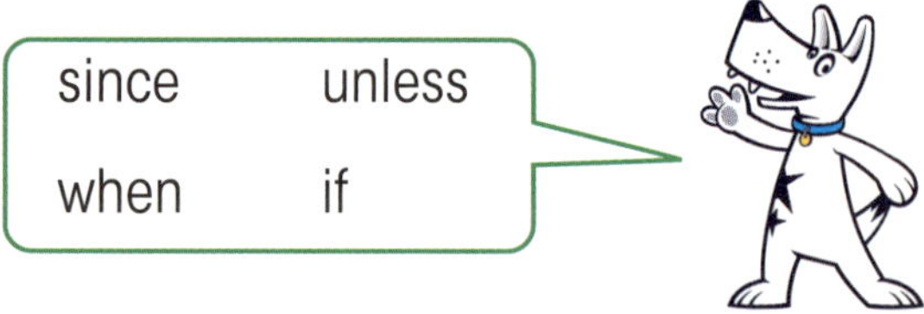

Look how they join the parts in these sentences:

*I have been having so much fun **since** you got here.*

*I can't play outside **unless** I wear my coat.*

*I wear my mittens **when** it is cold outside.*

*You can watch television **if** you finish your homework.*

These conjunctions connect one part of a sentence that makes sense on its own and another part that does not make sense on its own.

They are special because they can be used at the start or in the middle of a sentence:

Since *you got here, I have been having so much fun.*

Unless *I wear my coat, I can't play outside.*

When *it is cold outside, I wear my mittens.*

If *you finish your homework, you can watch television.*

Practice questions

1. Circle the conjunction.

   I haven't seen my uncle since we lived in Hong Kong.

2. Circle the word needed to finish the sentence. ***if*** ***when*** ***unless***

   I felt unhappy _____ my mum said I couldn't go to the party.

---

1. Circle the conjunction.

   I will be in trouble unless I can get all my work finished.

2. Circle the word needed to finish the sentence. ***if*** ***since*** ***when***

   My foot has been hurting _____ I tripped over.

3. Rewrite the misspelt word correctly.

   I like orange joose. [ ]

4. Circle the words that make ***you've***.

   have you   you of   you have

5. Make a new word. ***sub*** ***inter*** ***super***

   [ ]hero

6. Circle the plural form of ***goose***.

   gooses   geese   goose

7. The opposite of ***dead*** is [ ].

8. Which word? ***there*** ***their*** ***they're***

   Mum said _____ very wealthy.

9. Add ***was*** and ***were***.

   I [ ] *amazed when we* [ ] *in Paris.*

10. Add two capital letters.

    new delhi is a very busy city.

11. Add speech marks.

    When will the band come on stage? she asked.

12. Circle the missing adjective. ***delayed*** ***exciting***

    Yesterday, I watched a really _____ film.

Day 2

1. Circle the conjunction.

   We will go for a bike ride unless it starts raining.

2. Circle the word needed to finish the sentence. ***since*** ***when***

   I like to look out the window ______ it is snowing.

3. Add the word with the correct spelling. ***ckemist*** ***chemist***

   I went to the ______ to get my medicine.

4. Circle the rhyming words.

   juice loose grace

5. Add ***ment*** to make a new word.

   happy enjoy ______

6. Circle the plural form of ***pearl***.

   pearls pearles pearlies

7. The opposite of ***last*** is ______.

8. ***your*** or ***you're***?

   Don't forget to take ______ hat.

9. ***did*** or ***done***?

   I ______ a painting at school.

10. Add punctuation.

    greg said he saw joanne at the park today

11. Add speech marks.

    Would you like a drink? the waiter asked.

12. Circle the adjective.

    Sam played a new game.

Day 3

WEEK 25

1. Circle the conjunction.

   I will pack away my toys since I have finished playing with them.

2. Circle the word needed to finish the sentence. ***if*** ***since*** ***unless***

   I asked her ______ she had finished her work.

3. Rewrite the misspelt word correctly.

   I can't see through the wyndoe because it is dirty. ______

4. Circle the letters that are left out of the shortened words. ***could've***

   ca ha wi

5. Make a new word. ***inter*** ***super***

   ______view

6. Write the plural form of ***doctor***. ______

7. The opposite of ***hate*** is ______.

8. Add ***there***, ***their*** and ***they're***.

   See the people over ______?

   ______ having lunch and

   ______ food looks tasty!

9. ***was*** or ***were***?

   We ______ taking the dogs for a walk.

10. Add two capital letters.

    aisling and i like to read comics.

11. Add speech marks.

    Did you walk the dog? asked Mum.

12. Circle the adjectives.

    The slow, old computer annoyed Jane.

WEEK 25

Day 4

1. Circle the conjunction.

   We bought ice cream since it was such a hot day.

2. Circle the word needed to finish the sentence. ***if*** ***since*** ***when***

   I am happy _____ it is my birthday soon.

3. Add the word with the correct spelling. ***sundenlee*** ***suddenly***

   The balloon burst [ ].

4. Circle two words that rhyme with ***gnome***.

   foam know home

5. Make this word mean the opposite by changing the ending.
   less ***ness*** ***ment***

   hopeful [ ]

6. Write the singular form of ***envelopes***. [ ]

7. The opposite of ***coming*** is [ ].

8. ***Your*** or ***You're***?

   [ ] *very helpful!*

9. ***have*** or ***of***?

   Half [ ] *the food has been eaten.*

10. Add punctuation.

    my friends helped me pack up my things when i had to go

11. Add speech marks.

    Would you like any sauce? the lady asked.

12. Circle the adjective.

    Banjo is a friendly dog.

MY SCORE

Day 5

1. Circle the conjunction.

   My grandma lets us bake cakes when it is raining outside.

2. Circle the word needed to finish the sentence. ***if*** ***since*** ***when***

   I can go to the park _____ I have finished my homework.

3. Add the word with the correct spelling. ***prinse*** ***princess***

   The beautiful [ ] *put on her crown.*

4. Shorten ***might have***. [ ]

5. Make a new word. ***inter*** ***super***

   [ ]natural

6. Write the plural form of ***boat***.

   [ ]

7. The opposite of ***low*** is [ ].

8. ***its*** or ***it's***?

   Look, [ ] *snowing outside!*

9. ***was*** or ***were***?

   Sarah [ ] *on time today.*

10. Add capital letters.

    the solomon islands are in the pacific ocean.

11. Add speech marks.

    How are you? George asked politely.

12. Circle the missing adjective.
    helpful ***naughty***

    The lady thanked the _____ child.

MY SCORE

Skill focus

Rules for adding *ly*

Sometimes, groups of letters are added to the end of words.

This makes a new word which has a different meaning from the **base word**.

We usually add ***ly*** to the end of an adjective.

The new word is used to describe a verb or tell how an action was done:

run ***quickly*** *eat* ***slowly*** *sing* ***loudly***

For most words, we just add ***ly*** to the end of the word.

However, there are some words that do not follow this rule:

For words ending with ***y***, change the ***y*** to ***i*** and add ***ly***:	happ~~y~~ly (i) = happily
For words ending with ***le***, change the ***le*** to ***ly***:	simp~~le~~ (ly) = simply
For words ending with ***ic***, add ***ally***:	magic(+ally) = magically
For words ending with ***l***, add ***ly***:	wonderful(+ly) = wonderfully

Practice questions

1. Add ***ly*** to these words.
   (a) terrific + ly =
   (b) lazy + ly =
   (c) hopeful + ly =
   (d) noble + ly =

Day 1

1. Add ***ly*** to this word.
   quiet + ***ly*** =
2. Which one is not a word?
   roughly sadly shoutly
3. Add the word with the correct spelling. ***character*** ***karakter***
   My favourite cartoon character is Mickey Mouse.
4. Make a new word. ***mis*** ***inter***
   ______ national
5. ***express*** + ***ion*** =
6. Circle the plural of ***ferry***.
   ferrys ferries
7. Which word is NOT the opposite of ***catch***?
   release trap free
8. Add ***be*** and ***bee*** in the correct places.
   ______ *careful around that*
   ______ *or you might get stung.*
9. ***go***, ***goes*** or ***gone***?
   Joseph ______ *to language classes every week.*
10. Rewrite in the correct order and punctuate.
    favourite likes horse carrots my
11. Circle ***Gemmas*** or ***Gemma's***.
    ______ *cat had seven kittens last night.*
12. Circle the conjunction.
    We will go to the beach tomorrow, unless it is raining.

Day 2

1. Add **ly** to this word.

   easy + ***ly*** = [ ]

2. Which one is not a word?

   happily busily worrily

3. Circle and rewrite the misspelt word.

   The quizmaster asked a difficult queshun. [ ]

4. Make a new word. ***inter*** ***super***

   [ ]star

5. What is the correct spelling for ***tense*** + ***ion***? [ ]

6. Write the singular form of ***peaches***.

   [ ]

7. Which word is NOT similar in meaning to ***rapid***?

   fast terror quick

8. Circle the correct word. ***tale*** ***tail***

   The dog's _____ was wagging furiously.

9. ***was*** or ***were***?

   Mum and Dad [ ] *in the garden.*

10. Cross out the word that doesn't belong.

    I think looking after the nature is important.

11. Add punctuation.

    why isnt there any snow falling this winter

12. Circle the conjunction.

    Ross doesn't like dogs because he was bitten by one.

MY SCORE

Day 3

1. Add **ly** to this word.

   gentle + ***ly*** = [ ]

2. Which one is not a word?

   wobbly candly prickly

3. Rewrite the misspelt word correctly.

   My litle brother is only three. [ ]

4. Make this word mean the opposite.

   auto ***anti***

   [ ]freeze

5. Which one is not a word?

   action discussion quietion

6. Circle the singular form of ***cities***.

   citie city citee

7. Which word is NOT the opposite of ***several***?

   many none few

8. Write the correct word. ***rose*** ***rows***

   I chose one beautiful red flower from the many [ ] *of bushes.*

9. Circle the missing word. ***am is are***

   They _____ baking a birthday cake.

10. Rewrite in the correct order and punctuate.

    tiny sang the bird sweetly

    [ ]

11. Circle the correct one.

    The dogs are eating.

    The dog's are barking.

12. Circle the conjunction.

    Janine takes her dog for a walk each day when she gets home from work.

MY SCORE

WEEK 26

Day 4

1. Add *ly* to this word.
   music + *ly* = ☐

2. Which one is not a word?
   fantastically   terrifically   picnically

3. Circle and rewrite the misspelt word.
   The wimmen were chatting in the coffee shop. ☐

4. Pick. ***auto*** ***anti***
   The famous singer gave me his ☐graph.

5. What is the correct spelling for ***act*** + ***ion***? ☐

6. Write the plural form of ***fox***.
   ☐

7. Which word is NOT similar in meaning to ***invented***?
   made   created   captured

8. Circle the correct word. ***rain*** ***reign***
   The ______ watered the flowers in the garden.

9. ***was*** or ***were***?
   They ☐ *playing football.*

10. Cross out the word that doesn't belong.
    I'd rather not to meet you so early.

11. Punctuate.
    we didnt get to see the tigers at the zoo

12. Circle the conjunction.
    Jessie pulled up some carrots but her sister collected beans.

MY SCORE

Day 5

1. Add *ly* to this word.
   awful + *ly* = ☐

2. Which one is not a word?
   cheerfully   beautifully   untilly

3. Circle and rewrite the misspelt word.
   I like playing rock, paper, sissors with my friends. ☐

4. Add. ***auto*** ***anti***
   An ☐biography is a book someone writes about himself/herself.

5. Which one is not a word?
   division   invasion   paradsion

6. Circle the plural form of ***dairy***.
   dairys   dairies

7. Which word is NOT the opposite of ***valuable***?
   useless   cheap   expensive

8. Write the correct word. ***where*** ***wear***
   Do you know ☐ *to buy the dress she will* ☐ *for the party?*

9. ***seen*** or ***saw***?
   Have you ☐ *a koala before?*

10. Circle which word doesn't belong.
    Shall we will go and have lunch?

11. Write the missing word. ***cat's*** ***cats***
    Granny has four ☐ *outside.*

12. Circle the conjunction.
    My sister makes me laugh when she pulls funny faces.

Skill focus

Words that tell us where

There are special words that tell us about where people, places and things are, or are going.

Some of these words are:

above, along, around, at, behind, below, beside, between, down, into, in front of, from, near, on, out, over, past, through, towards, under

Using these words in a sentence makes it more detailed and interesting.

For example, instead of saying:

The girl walked.

You could use the word ***into*** to add more detail about where she walked:

The girl walked ***into*** *a dark and creepy cave.*

Practice questions

1. Underline the words that tell where the dog is.

   The dog is on the chair.

2. Circle the better word. ***over*** ***under***

   The horse jumped _____ the tall bush.

Day 1

1. Underline the words that tell where the pieces were put.

   I put the pieces in the box.

2. Circle the better word. ***beside*** ***into***

   He dived _____ the pool.

3. Add the word with the correct spelling. ***obai*** ***obey***

   My dog doesn't [ ] *my mum's commands.*

4. Circle the next word in alphabetical order.

   indicate interest inside increase

5. ***know*** + ***ing*** + ***ly*** = [ ]

6. Add the correct form of ***high***.

   I jumped the [ ] *in today's competition.*

7. Circle the closest meaning to ***collection***.

   variety bewildered imagine

8. Circle the opposite of ***boring***.

   interesting plain dull

9. Circle the missing word. ***Where's*** ***Where'll***

   _____ *the key to the garden shed?*

10. Circle which word doesn't belong.

    My friend, Janine, comes from in Germany.

11. The kite belongs to [ ].

    Jim's kite flew the highest.

12. Add the words in the correct places. ***bread*** ***rice***

    slices of [ ]

    grains of [ ]

MY SCORE

Day 2

1. Underline the words that tell where she lives.

   She lives by the river.

2. Circle the better word. ***towards on***

   I rode my bike _____ the school.

3. Circle and rewrite the misspelt word.

   The ants walked in a perfectly strate line.

4. Write in alphabetical order.

   potatoes possible porridge

5. Which one is not a word?

   usually naturally deally

6. Change the ending to make this word mean the ***most friendly***.

   friendlier

7. Circle the closest meaning to ***instantly***.

   symbol immediately location

8. Circle the opposite of ***similar***.

   alike different same

9. Write a different word that sounds similar to ***line*** (*Hint: animal*).

10. Circle which word doesn't belong.

    I'd rather not to go out tonight, I'm too tired.

11. Circle the correct one.

    Jame's jumper. Gran's handbag.

12. Write the word that correctly completes the sentence.
    bat squirrel owl

    We found an _____ asleep in our tree house.

MY SCORE

Day 3

1. Underline the words that tell where the puppies slept.

   The puppies slept on their mat.

2. Circle the better word. ***near through***

   The car went _____ the tunnel.

3. Write the jumbled word correctly.

   I walked along the warnor path.

4. Number in alphabetical order.

   though thought through

5. Circle the correct spelling of ***basic*** + ***ly***.

   basically basicly

6. Add the correct form of ***new***.

   My bike is _____ than my sister's.

7. The closest meaning to ***attempt*** is:

   start finish try

8. Circle the opposite of ***past***.

   when future sometimes

9. Circle the missing word.
   hadn't couldn't

   Mum _____ finished making dinner when the guests arrived.

10. Circle which word doesn't belong.

    My friend Bill went under to the cinema last night.

11. The books belong to _____.

    The children's books.

12. Add the words in the correct places. ***tea milk***

    cups of _____

    bottles of _____

MY SCORE

WEEK 27

WEEK 27

Day 4

1. Underline the words that tell where the juice is.

   The juice is in the fridge.

2. Circle the better word. ***on*** ***around***

   I left my book _____ the bench.

3. Add the word with the correct spelling. ***inuff*** ***enough***

   I made [ ] cake for everyone to share.

4. Write in alphabetical order.

   guess guide guard

   [ ] [ ] [ ]

5. ***angry*** + ***ly***? [ ]

6. Change the ending to make this word mean the ***most lovely***.

   lovelier [ ]

7. Circle the closest meaning to ***emperor***.

   ancient guard king

8. Circle the opposite of ***problem***.

   solution primary

9. Write a word that sounds the same as ***some***. (*Hint: +, x*)

   [ ]

10. Circle which word doesn't belong.

    I put in the pieces in the box.

11. Circle the missing word. ***Nevilles*** ***Neville's***

    Where are _____ shoes?

12. Circle the word that correctly completes the sentence. ***cheese*** ***steak*** ***egg***

    Roger fried an _____ for his lunch.

MY SCORE

Day 5

1. Underline the words that tell where the note was put.

   Put the note on the fridge.

2. Circle the better word. ***out*** ***over***

   The birds flew _____ the buildings.

3. Circle and rewrite the misspelt word.

   The treats were shared amoung the children. [ ]

4. Number in alphabetical order.

   chord [ ] choir [ ] chorus [ ]

5. Which one is not a word?

   gently simply fastly

6. Add the correct form of ***big***.

   My mum gave me the [ ] of the four cupcakes.

7. Circle the word closest in meaning to ***afraid***.

   helpful brave frightened

8. Circle the opposite of ***wet***.

   dry damp warm

9. Add the missing word. ***didn't*** ***don't***

   The dog [ ] finish its dinner last night.

10. Circle which word doesn't belong.

    Yesterday, Gina could be competing in the Olympics some day.

11. Circle the missing word. ***cupboard's*** ***cupboards***

    We have five _____ in our kitchen.

12. Which word correctly completes the sentence? ***potatoes*** ***steaks*** ***pasta***

    Jenny peeled the _____.

MY SCORE

Why do we add *in-* to words?

Sometimes, groups of letters are added to the beginning of words.

This makes a new word which has a different meaning from the **base word**.

The word part ***in*** usually means ***not***. It makes the base word its opposite:

✓ correct ⟶ ✗ incorrect

We can usually just add ***in*** to the start of the word.

However, there are some words that don't follow this rule:

When the word starts with an ***l***, ***in*** changes to ***il***:	~~in~~ (il) + legal = illegal
When the word starts with an ***m*** or ***p***, ***in*** changes to ***im***:	~~in~~ (im) + mature = immature ~~in~~ (im) + perfect = imperfect
When the word starts with an ***r***, ***in*** changes to ***ir***:	~~in~~ (ir) + responsible = irresponsible

Practice questions

Make these words mean the opposite.

il im ir in

(a) ______ secure

(b) ______ patient

(c) ______ regular

(d) ______ logical

1. Make this word mean the opposite.
   il ***im*** ***ir*** ***in***
   ______ possible

2. Is the word used correctly?
   yes ☐ no ☐
   That's easy to do. It's <u>impossible</u>!

3. Add the word with the correct spelling. ***Hello*** ***Helow***
   '______', said the friendly boy.

4. Circle the two rhyming words.
   guide died hiding

5. Add ***ly*** to make a new word.
   simple city echo ______

6. Add the correct form of ***eat***.
   My cat ______ its dinner.

7. Circle the close meanings.
   blue navy gold

8. Add ***cereal*** or ***serial***.
   I like to eat ______.

9. ***was*** or ***were***?
   Johanna ______ born in Germany.

10. Add two commas.
    The plane flew over Indonesia India Iran and Iraq.

11. Underline the words that tell where she put the banana.
    The lady put the banana in her lunch box.

12. Circle the tense this sentence is written in. ***past*** ***present*** ***future***
    Ann planted flowers in the garden.

MY SCORE ☐

WEEK 28

Day 2

1. Make this word mean the opposite.

il im ir in [ ]correct

2. Is the word used correctly?

yes [ ] no [ ]

I got all the questions right. They were incorrect.

3. Add the word with the correct spelling. ***suppose*** ***supows***

I [ ] you may have one more biscuit.

4. Circle the word you can add to ***line***.

on fish

5. Circle the correct spelling of ***different*** + ***ly***.

differenttly differently

6. Change the ending to make this word mean the ***most hot***.

hotter [ ]

7. Circle the opposites.

spend buy save

8. Add ***air*** or ***heir***.

The [ ] in the city was quite polluted.

9. ***I*** or ***me***?

When I grow up I'd like people to watch [ ] act in plays.

10. Add punctuation.

the small child threw a tantrum

11. Circle the better word. ***on*** ***with***

Sandra's car is blue ___ a white roof.

12. Circle the tense this sentence is written in. ***past*** ***present*** ***future***

We played basketball yesterday.

MY SCORE

Day 3

1. Make this word mean the opposite.

il im ir in [ ]legal

2. Is the word used correctly?

yes [ ] no [ ]

When you break the law you are doing something illegal.

3. Rewrite the misspelt word correctly.

We were just in time for the konsert! [ ]

4. Circle the rhyming words.

glue two so

5. What is the correct spelling for ***noble*** + ***ly***? [ ]

6. Write the correct form of ***bring***.

Mr Field [ ] his pet pig to school today.

7. Circle the close meanings.

river stream sea

8. Add ***tea*** or ***tee***.

I made Mum a pot of [ ].

9. ***was*** or ***were***?

Tom [ ] at my house last night.

10. Add two commas.

Hurling soccer football and rugby are sports played in Ireland.

11. Underline the words that tell where he left his bag.

He left his bag next to his bike.

12. Circle the tense this sentence is written in. ***past*** ***present*** ***future***

I bought my sister a teddy bear for her birthday.

MY SCORE

Day 4

1. Make this word mean the opposite.

   il im ir in [ ]regular

2. Is the word used correctly?

   yes [ ] no [ ]

   His broken arm was bent in an irregular way.

3. Write the jumbled word correctly.

   A big psriures party was held for Dad's 40th birthday.

   [ ]

4. Circle the word you can add to ***cut***.

   meat hair

5. ***hope*** + ***less*** + ***ly*** = [ ]

6. Change the ending to make this word mean the ***most dear***.

   dearer [ ]

7. Circle the opposites.

   fierce calm dirty

8. Add ***weak*** or ***week***.

   There are seven days in a [ ].

9. ***I*** or ***Me***?

   [ ] *don't like centipedes.*

10. Add punctuation.

    jen gave laura a present

11. Circle the better word. ***on*** ***off***

    I took the washing ___ the line.

12. Circle the tense this sentence is written in. ***past*** ***present*** ***future***

    I will visit my grandparents this weekend.

MY SCORE

Day 5

1. Make this word mean the opposite.

   il im ir in [ ]mortal

2. Is the word used correctly?

   yes [ ] no [ ]

   Someone who lives forever is immortal.

3. Rewrite the misspelt word correctly.

   Kevin tryed to cook pancakes at the weekend.

4. Circle the rhyming words.

   chewing doing sewing

5. Add ***ly*** to make a new word.

   start true face [ ]

6. Add the correct form of ***read*** to the sentence.

   Dad was [ ] *to his children.*

7. Circle the close meanings.

   entrance information knowledge

8. Add ***hour*** or ***our***.

   That cake baked for an [ ].

9. ***was*** or ***were***?

   I [ ] *late this morning.*

10. Add commas.

    I cut apples bananas oranges and grapes for the fruit salad.

11. Underline the words that tell where they walked.

    The choir walked across the stage.

12. Circle the tense this sentence is written in. ***past*** ***present*** ***future***

    Samara will be going to France for a holiday.

WEEK 29

Skill focus

Commas for places

A **comma** is a type of mark used in sentences to show a short pause.

This helps make the meaning of a sentence clearer.

A comma looks like this:

Commas are often used between the separate parts of a place. For example:

*My aunt lives in **Darwin, Australia**.*

A comma is used here to separate the city (Darwin) and the country (Australia).

Practice questions

1. Add a comma to separate the city and the country.

   The Leaning Tower of Pisa is in Pisa Italy.

2. Tick the correct punctuation.

   The first hamburgers were made in ____.

   (a) , Hamburg Germany ☐

   (b) Hamburg, Germany ☐

Day 1

1. Add a comma to separate the city and the country.

   The Eiffel Tower is in Paris France.

2. The Trevi Fountain is in ____.

   Rome, Italy ☐

   Rome Italy ☐

3. Write the jumbled word correctly.

   The train otanist was full of people. ☐

4. Shorten ***did not***. ☐

5. Add two letters to make a word that means ***not correct***.

   ☐correct

6. Circle the plural form of ***knife***.

   knifes knives

7. Circle the opposite of ***hardworking***.

   lazy bored energetic

8. Circle the missing word. ***too to two***

   I woke up ____ early this morning.

9. Write the missing word.
   didn't hasn't

   Kieran ☐ *finished his breakfast yet.*

10. Add punctuation.

    Mercury Venus Mars and Jupiter are planets

11. Pick the better word. ***work works***

    Mike's dad ☐ *all over the world.*

12. Circle a past tense form of ***he flies***.

    he flew he flyed he flown

Day 2

1. Add a comma to separate the city and the country.

   The Pyramid of Giza is in Cairo Egypt.

2. Tick the correct punctuation.
   The Eiffel Tower is in ____.

   , Paris France ▢

   Paris, France ▢

3. Circle and rewrite the misspelt word.

   I am in the blue spelling groop. ▢

4. Circle the two rhyming words.

   tray they key

5. Add two letters to make a word that means ***not perfect***.

   im in ir il ▢perfect

6. Write the plural form of ***mouse***.

   ▢

7. Circle the word closest in meaning to ***chat***.

   scream speak shout

8. Which word? ***there their they're***

   I really like ____ house!

9. Circle the missing word.
   hasn't wasn't

   Sally ____ seen her grandparents for a year.

10. Add punctuation.

    have you seen big ben in london

11. Underline the words that tell where she rode.

    Zoe rode her bike around the park.

12. Command ▢, question ▢ or statement ▢?

    Where is your sister?

MY SCORE

Day 3

1. Add a comma.

   Saint Basil's is a famous cathedral in Moscow Russia.

2. Tick the correct punctuation.
   The Pyramid of Giza is in ____.

   Cairo, Egypt ▢ Cairo Egypt ▢

3. Circle the word that is spelt correctly. ***crept creept***

   The cat ____ silently.

4. Add the negative form of ***can***.

   Dogs ▢ *talk, but some birds can.*

5. Add two letters to make a word that means ***not active***.

   il im in ir ▢active

6. Circle the plural form of ***leaf***.

   leaves leafs

7. Circle the opposite of ***find***.

   lose search seek

8. ***by***, ***bye*** or ***buy***?

   I need to ▢ *some milk.*

9. Add the missing word. ***didn't don't***

   Phil ▢ *come to the beach with us.*

10. Add punctuation.

    deer squirrels rabbits and foxes live in the forest

11. Circle the correct word. ***lives live***

    Whales ____ in the sea.

12. Circle the present tense.

    They were saying.

    They are saying.

    They is saying.

WEEK 29

Day 4

1. Add a comma.

   The Statue of Liberty is in New York USA.

2. Tick the correct punctuation.
   The Opera House is in ____.

   Sydney, Australia ◯

   , Sydney Australia ◯

3. Circle and rewrite the misspelt word.

   My friend comes to visit me offen. ▭

4. Circle the rhyming words.

   lose choose those

5. Add two letters to make a word that means ***not patient***.

   il im in ir ▭patient

6. Write the singular form of ***women***.

   ▭

7. Circle the word closest in meaning to ***tired***.

   exhausted exit energetic

8. Which word? ***there their they're***

   What's ▭ *last name?*

9. Add the missing word. ***hasn't wasn't***

   I'm glad it ▭ *raining.*

10. Add punctuation.

    where are your brothers and sisters living

11. Where did they dance? Circle it.

    The circus perfomers danced across the tightrope.

12. Command ◯, question ◯ or statement ◯?

    Go and choose a book to read.

MY SCORE

Day 5

1. Add a comma to separate the city and country.

   Big Ben is located in London England.

2. Tick the correct punctuation.
   The Statue of Liberty is in ____.

   New, York USA ◯ New York, USA ◯

3. Write the jumbled word correctly.

   August is the htgieh month of the year. ▭

4. Shorten ***must not***. ▭

5. Add two letters to make a word that means ***not responsible***.

   il im in ir ▭responsible

6. Circle the plural form of ***wolf***.

   wolfs wolves

7. Circle the opposite of ***cheap***.

   costly free young

8. Add ***pale*** or ***pail*** to the sentence.

   The dress was a ▭ *blue.*

9. Write the missing word.
   hadn't couldn't

   Rebecca ▭ *play tennis because she broke her arm.*

10. Add punctuation.

    we need ham cheese and pineapple to make pizzas

11. Circle the correct word.
    make makes

    Cats and dogs ____ good pets.

12. Circle a past tense form of ***brings***.

    has brought has brung has bringed

MY SCORE

More speech marks

Speech marks are used to show where the speaker's words begin and end.

Often, we are told who is speaking at the beginning or end of their speech:

__Tom said__, 'Watch out for the bees!'

'Watch out for the bees!' __said Tom__.

When the same person has said more than one sentence, the speech may continue after we are told who the speaker is:

Remember, the speech marks hold the words that are *actually* said by the speaker.

The words that tell us who is speaking do not go inside the speech marks.

Practice questions

1. Add speech marks.
   Do you know where my book is? Jane asked her mum. I can't find it anywhere!

2. Are the speech marks used correctly? *yes* ☐ *no* ☐
   'My friend is having a party tomorrow, said Susan. I can't wait to go!'

---

1. Add speech marks.
   Laura! Mum called. It's time to come inside!

2. Are the speech marks used correctly? yes ☐ no ☐
   'Look at that dog', said Elliot. 'He has a fluffy tail!'

3. Circle and rewrite the misspelt word.
   I don't see you often enuff. ☐

4. Number in alphabetical order.
   noodle ☐ normal ☐ nobody ☐

5. Add two letters to make a word that means ***not polite***.
   il im in ir ☐polite

6. Circle the plural form of ***picture***.
   pictures pictuires

7. Which word is NOT similar in meaning to ***letter***?
   drawing postcard note

8. Which word means ***to press and stretch dough***?
   need knead

9. ***did*** or ***done***?
   She has ☐ *her washing;* ☐ *you finish yours?*

10. Add capital letters.
    my friend niall is from new zealand.

11. Add punctuation.
    Amy was born in madrid spain

12. Circle the conjunction.
    Rory runs every day because it's good for his health.

MY SCORE ☐

WEEK 30

Day 2

1. Add speech marks.

   Quickly! James said. Let's go now!

2. Are the speech marks used correctly? yes ▢ no ▢

   'Yes, please!' shouted the small child. 'I want an ice cream!'

3. Rewrite the misspelt word correctly.

   That's not trew! ▢

4. Circle the two rhyming words.

   left lift shift

5. Circle the correct spelling of ***begin*** + ***er***.

   beginner beginer

6. Circle the singular of ***bicycles***.

   ▢

7. Which word is NOT the opposite of ***everybody***?

   none everyone nobody

8. Which word means to ***pull along***?

   toe tow

9. ***was*** or ***were***?

   It ▢ *lunchtime and we* ▢ *hungry!*

10. Add capital letters.

    the south pole is in antarctica.

11. Add commas.

    I took my towel flippers mask and snorkel to the beach.

12. Circle the conjunction.

    Our dogs are very afraid of thunder and lightning.

MY SCORE

Day 3

1. Add speech marks.

   You look sad! Tara said. What's wrong?

2. Are the speech marks used correctly? yes ▢ no ▢

   'Where is your sister? asked Mum.' 'She's in big trouble!'

3. Write the jumbled word correctly.

   There was no rpfoo that he was guilty. ▢

4. Write in alphabetical order.

   cork corn cold

   ▢ ▢ ▢

5. Pick. ***re*** ***in***

   I will ▢ *decorate my house.*

6. Write the plural of ***sponge***.

   ▢

7. Which word is NOT similar in meaning to ***tear***?

   split fix rip

8. Which word means a ***group of cattle***?

   heard herd

9. ***did*** or ***done***?

   I ▢ *my homework. Have you* ▢ *yours?*

10. Add two capital letters.

    my mum's name is jen.

11. Add punctuation.

    i live in brazil south america

12. Circle the conjunction.

    I'm good at drawing but I don't paint very well.

MY SCORE

WEEK 30

Day 4

1. Add speech marks.

   Mum! I called out. Where is my other sock?

2. Are the speech marks used correctly? yes ☐ no ☐

   'Do you have my ball? John asked' Jenny. 'I want it back!'

3. Rewrite the word correctly.

   I lurn Indonesian.

   ☐

4. Circle the two rhyming words.

   season reason person

5. Write the missing letters.

   danger ☐

6. Write the singular form of ***eyes***.

   ☐

7. Which word is NOT the opposite of ***glad***?

   upset happy depressed

8. Which word means a fruit?

   pair pear

9. ***was*** or ***were***?

   The children ☐ *dirty.*

10. Add two capital letters.

    My cousin, fee, lives in canada.

11. Add one comma.

    I saw Jo Sam and Tim at the shops.

12. Circle the conjunction.

    We ate fish and chips for dinner.

MY SCORE

Day 5

1. Add speech marks.

   Dinner's ready! yelled Dad. Come and get it!

2. Are the speech marks used correctly? yes ☐ no ☐

   'Please put on your hat, said Dad. Then go outside.'

3. Write the jumbled word correctly.

   The name of our planet is trhEa. ☐

4. Write in alphabetical order.

   fork forest forty

   ☐ ☐ ☐

5. Make this word mean the opposite.

   mis un dis ☐ important

6. Circle the plural form of ***name***.

   nameis names

7. Which word is NOT similar in meaning to ***vast***?

   huge reward enormous

8. Which word means ***correct***?

   right write

9. ***did*** or ***done***?

   What ☐ *you think of the school play?*

10. Add a capital letter.

    The longest river is the nile.

11. Add punctuation.

    We live in tokyo japan.

12. Circle the conjunction.

    The children got wet when it started to rain.

MY SCORE

WEEK 31

Skill focus

More than one owner

When we want to show that something belongs to someone, we use a small mark after the owner or owners and the letter ***s***.

The small mark is called an **apostrophe**. It looks like this:

The tail of the apostrophe always points to the owner or owners.

When there is more than one owner and that word already ends in ***s***, we must do something different.

We only add an apostrophe, not another ***s***.

Practice questions

1. Who do the dogs belong to?
   (a) the farmers ☐
   (b) a farmer ☐
   The farmers' dogs.
2. Add an apostrophe to show more than one owner.
   The painters brushes.

Day 1

1. Who do the hats belong to?
   the boys ☐ a boy ☐
   The boys' hats.
2. Add an apostrophe after the s to show more than one owner.
   The ducks pond.
3. Circle and rewrite the misspelt word.
   We stayed up untill midnight on New Year's Eve. ☐
4. Write in alphabetical order.
   buries built busy
   ☐ ☐ ☐
5. Circle the correct spelling of ***magic*** + ***ly***.
   magically magicly
6. Circle the plural of ***diary***.
   diaries diarys
7. Circle the word closest in meaning to ***naughty***.
   good bad kind
8. Write a word that sounds the same as ***pause***. (*Hint: dog or cat*)
   ☐
9. Circle the missing word.
   didn't ***don't***
   I ____ think it will rain today.
10. Add punctuation.
    i will be celebrating my birthday in bangkok thailand.
11. Circle the missing adjective.
    red ***orange***
    Mr Bakir's house has a ____ roof.
12. Circle the verb.
    The child ran clumsily.

Day 2

1. Who do the shoes belong to?
the girls ▢ a girl ▢
The girls' shoes.

2. Add an apostrophe after the s to show more than one owner.
The boys hats.

3. Circle and rewrite the misspelt word.
A sentury is one hundred years. ▢

4. Which word can be added to make a new word? ***tooth*** ***white***
▢ paste

5. Make this word mean the opposite.
il ***un***
▢ legal

6. Write the correct form of ***bring***.
Nan ▢ *treats for us when she visits.*

7. Circle the opposite of ***enemy***.
friend foe hate

8. Write a word that sounds the same as ***raise***. (*Hint: the sun's ...*)
▢

9. Circle the missing word(s).
am not ***isn't*** ***aren't***
I ____ happy with how my cake turned out.

10. Add speech marks.
There's no time! she called. You're going to miss the train!

11. ***a*** or ***an***?
▢ *excellent film*

12. Circle the verb group.
They are writing very neatly.

MY SCORE

Day 3

1. Who do the bags belong to?
the ladies ▢ a lady ▢
The ladies' bags.

2. Add an apostrophe after the s to show more than one owner.
The girls shoes.

3. Write the jumbled word correctly.
If we all go gehtoter we will have the best time. ▢

4. Write in alphabetical order.
button bottle bottom
▢ ▢ ▢

5. Circle the correct spelling of ***busy*** + ***ly***.
busyly busily

6. Circle the plural of ***worry***.
worrys worries

7. Circle the word closest in meaning to ***terrible***.
great awful scary

8. Write a word that sounds the same as ***would***. (*Hint: trees*)
▢

9. Circle the missing word(s).
am not ***isn't*** ***aren't***
They ____ going to make it.

10. Add punctuation.
we are going to tokyo japan

11. Circle the word that correctly completes the sentence.
funny ***interesting*** ***scary***
Kim watched an ____ TV show.

12. Circle the verb.
I spoke to my grandad on the phone.

WEEK 31

WEEK 31

Day 4

1. Who do the cars belong to?
   the racers ◯ a racer ◯
   The racers' cars.

2. Add an apostrophe after the s to show more than one owner.
   The ladies bags.

3. Circle and rewrite the misspelt word.
   I feel afraid of thunderstorms sumtimes. [ ]

4. Which word can be added to make a new word? ***print*** ***shoe***
   foot [ ]

5. Which one is not a word?
   inactive inright incorrect

6. Write the correct form of ***buy***.
   Yesterday, we [ ] *a lot of fruit at the market.*

7. Circle the opposite of ***happiness***.
   sadness weakness hopeless

8. Write a word that sounds the same as ***flower***. (*Hint: make cakes*)
   [ ]

9. Add the missing word(s).
   am not ***isn't*** ***aren't***
   She [ ] *coming to my party because she's sick.*

10. Add speech marks.
    Mum! called Sam. Where are you?

11. ***a*** or ***an***?
    [ ] *friendly person*

12. Circle the verb group.
    Mr Kelly's shop will be closing at eight o'clock.

MY SCORE

Day 5

1. Who do the eggs belong to?
   the chickens ◯ a chicken ◯
   The chickens' eggs.

2. Add an apostrophe after the s to show more than one owner.
   The racers cars.

3. Rewrite the misspelt word correctly.
   Danny wonted to watch the news at five. [ ]

4. Write in alphabetical order.
   cousin country couple
   [ ] [ ] [ ]

5. Circle the correct spelling of ***fantastic*** + ***ly***.
   fantastically fantasticly

6. Circle the plural of ***fairy***.
   fairys fairies

7. Circle the word closest in meaning to ***complete***.
   start finish try

8. Write a word that sounds the same as ***plane***. (*Hint: not fancy*)
   [ ]

9. Add the missing word(s).
   am not ***isn't*** ***aren't***
   You [ ] *going!*

10. Add punctuation.
    i live in hobart tasmania.

11. Which word correctly completes the sentence?
    luxury ***expensive*** ***beautiful***
    We stayed in an ____ hotel.

12. Circle the verb.
    My pet bird flew away.

MY SCORE

Day 1

1. Rewrite the misspelt word correctly.

   I can't beleeve you were late again! [ ]

2. Circle the rhyming words.

   palm part calm

3. Circle the word you can add to ***bike***.

   motor wheel

4. Add. ***dis*** ***un***

   I [ ] agree with what you are saying.

5. Change the ending to make this word mean the ***most dark***.

   darker [ ]

6. Circle the opposite of ***weakness***.

   special strength sentence

7. Circle the word closest in meaning to ***broken***.

   fixed destroyed dirtied

8. ***to***, ***too*** or ***two***?

   Let's take a rug [ ] sit on.

9. Who do the toys belong to?
   the babies [ ] a baby [ ]

   The babies' toys.

10. Add punctuation.

    id like to visit sweden and norway next year said Sian.

11. Circle the verb group.

    Pavol was laughing at the clown.

12. Circle the nouns.

    They have four cars and three bikes.

MY SCORE

Day 2

1. Write the jumbled word correctly.

   The magician made the card isdaperpa. [ ]

2. ***That'll*** means [ ].

3. Circle the word you can add to ***yard*** and ***house***.

   farm beach

4. What is the correct spelling for ***angry*** + ***ly***? [ ]

5. Write the singular form of ***witches***.

   [ ]

6. Circle the opposite of ***quietly***.

   noisily lightly juicy

7. Circle the word closest in meaning to ***woman***.

   gentleman lady boy

8. ***was*** or ***were***?

   Harriet [ ] eating grapes.

9. Add an apostrophe after the ***s*** to show more than one owner.

   The babies toys.

10. Add three capital letters.

    we will visit greece and croatia on our holiday.

11. Circle the correct word.
    quiet ***quietly***

    Mr Holmes spoke very ____.

12. Write the correct verb in the box.

    I cook. Jim [ ]. Jim and Jane cook.

WEEK 32

Day 3

1. Rewrite the misspelt word correctly.

   'What hapened?' Mum asked us.

2. Circle the rhyming words.

   though caught thought

3. Circle the word you can add to ***news***.

   paper carton

4. Add ***re*** to make a new word.

   possible continue appear

5. Change the ending to make this word mean the ***most dirty***.

   dirtier

6. Circle the opposite of ***continue***.

   move stop go

7. Circle the word closest in meaning to ***photo***.

   sketch picture cartoon

8. Circle the missing word. ***too to two***

   Take the dog ____ the vet.

9. Who do the books belong to?
   the librarians ☐ a librarian ☐

   The librarians' books.

10. Add punctuation.

    i wasnt ready for my race and i came in last

11. Circle the verb group.

    My baby brother will cry easily.

12. Circle the noun.

    The big city was busy.

MY SCORE

Day 4

1. Write the jumbled word correctly.

   Ring the door bell when you virrea.

2. ***Let's*** means ________.

3. Circle the word you can add to ***break***.

   fruit fast

4. Add ***ly*** to make a new word.

   gentle joke giant

5. Circle the plural form of ***crash***.

   crashes crashs

6. Circle the opposite of ***nervous***.

   calm scared worried

7. Circle the word closest in meaning to ***fall***.

   throw lift drop

8. ***was*** or ***were***?

   Jo and Kim ________ here earlier.

9. Add an apostrophe after the s to show more than one owner.

   The librarians books.

10. Add four capital letters.

    my friend, amir, lives in new york.

11. Circle the correct word.
    final finally

    Joe ____ finished the race.

12. Write the next verb.

    I walk. You walk.

    She ________.

MY SCORE

WEEK 32

Day 5

1. Add the word with the correct spelling. ***ordinry*** ***ordinary***

   He seems a very [ ] *man.*

2. Circle the two rhyming words.

   flare car wear

3. Circle the word you can add to ***sun***.

   week flower

4. Make this word mean the opposite. ***mis*** ***un*** ***dis***

   [ ]honest

5. Change the ending to make this word mean the ***most tasty***.

   tastier [ ]

6. Circle the opposite of ***float***.

   suck sink seek

7. Circle the word closest in meaning to ***shore***.

   mountain coast city

8. Which word? ***too*** ***to*** ***two***

   Take [ ] *cupcakes.*

9. Who do the paws belong to? the cats ◯ a cat ◯

   The cats' paws.

10. Add punctuation.

    dont forget to put the bin out! Mum reminded me

11. Circle the verb group.

    They are going home soon.

12. Circle the noun.

    The sad and lonely boy looked miserable.

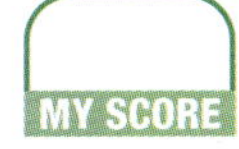

Skill focus review

1. Rewrite the misspelt word correctly.

   'That's enuff TV for tonight', said Mum. [ ]

2. Circle ***hadn't*** or ***couldn't***.

   Sarah ____ see the screen properly.

3. Circle the two rhyming words.

   vein cane dine

4. Make this word mean the opposite. ***il*** ***im*** ***ir*** ***in***

   [ ]formal

5. Add ***ly*** to make a new word.

   crazy count cash

   [ ]

6. The opposite of ***early*** is [ ].

7. Add a comma.

   My pen pal lives in San Diego California.

8. Add an apostrophe after the s to show more than one owner.

   The rabbits hutches.

9. Who do the cats belong to? the girls ◯ a girl ◯

   The girls' cats.

10. Add speech marks.

    I can't wait to get home! said Liam excitedly. It's my birthday!

11. Circle the conjunction.

    I will be late for school unless I can be ready in five minutes.

12. Underline the words that tell where Jill lived.

    Jill lived near the school.

NOTES

NOTES

NOTES